WHEN YOU ⎰

a personal exploration of life,
suffering and belief

Philip Wetherell

GILEAD
B O O K S

Gilead Books Publishing
Corner Farm
West Knapton
Malton
North Yorkshire YO17 8JB
www.GileadBooksPublishing.com

First published in Great Britain, 16th July 2011
Reprinted June 2012

2 4 6 8 10 9 7 5 3

British Library Cataloguing-in-Publication Data:
A catalogue record for this book is available from the British Library.

ISBN-13: 978-0-9568560-0-5

Cover photo © Paul Bryden
Cover design: Nathan Ward

CONTENTS

INTERNATIONAL COMMENDATIONS:

'Facing death is not an easy matter. Not when your days are counted. Not when it is evident your body is deteriorating, and your will to fight slowly diminishes. Not when all you can do is to take a deep breath and a defiant stand before God for his apparent absence from a depraved world, a world that moves adrift in the overall scheme of creation. Not when this defiant stand betrays a sense of nostalgia for someone who is no longer there. Side by side with Gaby, his wife, Philip has written a poignant story. His book will touch many a reader, regardless of his or her own condition. This is so because it is written with the passion of a heart that is dying against his will and because the writer wants his words of wisdom about his own experience of life and death to last and to survive him. This is why I highly recommend reading this exceptional book.'
Elsa Tamez, Emeritus Professor of the Latin American Biblical University

'We thank God for Philip's practical vision on many issues touching human life. Working in different positions in USPG for many years he was able to engage with the World Church and help various parts thereof to engage with each other. I saw Philip in Mozambique and in London and he showed to be very much engaged. His book will be a faithful witness of what he meant to many.'
Bishop Dinis Sengulane of Lebombo, Mozambique

'Philip was a special person. He helped greatly in missionary work in South West Brazil when he visited here as Anglican Secretary. In USPG he was a faithful companion. His kindness and caring have always been a complement to his seriousness. God gave him this destiny mysteriously soon. To him and his dear Gaby we owe our honour and our gratitude.'
Bishop Jubal Neves of South Western Brazil

FOREWORD

I believe this to be a very significant book. It is a moving yet unsentimental account of the last few months in the life of a man, Philip Wetherell, who was suddenly diagnosed as having Motor Neurone Disease. He died before the book was completed, by which time he was almost totally paralysed and the book was being written a single letter at a time with the aid of eye movements and a computer. It was completed by Gaby, Philip's wife and former colleague, and latterly his carer.

Philip writes with transparent honesty about life and death, pain and suffering, faith and fear. His priestly ministry had taken Philip, through the mission agency he served, to many parts of the globe; but he and Gaby had also been rooted for some years in an inner city south London parish. All this is part of the mix which helps Philip to reflect, theologically and with humanity, upon his situation. One of the most significant sections is that which describes precisely what it is like to live with a disease which gets progressively more severe. He explains that every miracle of medical technology which aids the sufferer can also be seen as a sign that the situation is becoming worse. Another important section is that on assisted suicide – because for Philip of course this was no theoretical issue. He rigorously examines the arguments against this but concludes that he feels that the Church is mistaken in opposing it, although stating that he does not know whether he would have the courage himself to request it. He also records that, from his own situation, he is aware that things can change from day to day partly through the effect of certain drugs.

Towards the end Philip records that he was totally dependent on others and felt unable to give them anything in return, except this book! It is his final gift to those who knew him, loved and admired him, and it is a gift well worth having. Uniquely we have a thoughtful record from inside the mind of a priest and a man approaching death in the most difficult of circumstances. Everyone will be enriched through reading this book.

+Tom Butler
(Former Bishop of Southwark)

PREFACE

The worst moment of my life was in July 2007, when my husband, Philip Wetherell, was diagnosed with Motor Neurone Disease; worse even than the moment he died. The only mitigating factor when hearing the diagnosis was that we received it together. The three years between those two moments were very hard for both of us and we used different strategies to cope with what was happening.

For Philip, the knowledge that his time was suddenly limited spurred him to put down in writing his questions, thoughts and beliefs on a wide variety of issues which were important to him – matters of life and death – and this book is the result. The initial draft included chapters on subjects as diverse as Community, Christians and Other Faiths, Peace, Homophobia and Africa. He omitted these from the final manuscript but they are available as downloads from www.GileadBooksPublishing.com.

Philip would not have described himself as a theologian but he was always an avid researcher and a gifted preacher. Because of his paralysis, proper research was latterly impossible but his preacher's heart kept him doggedly struggling to get his thoughts onto the computer. He used the prison of his illness to dig deeply into the Bible, into his experience of the world and into his own heart, testing his own and other people's beliefs. Since he died I have been assisted by many dear friends in refining and editing his writing. This was especially necessary for Chapters 9 and 13, both of which were left unfinished. They therefore now contain some material from earlier writings which I have grafted into his original drafts. In the case of Chapter 9 this includes parts of the Community chapter mentioned above.

In early July 2010 Philip lost the ability to control even the muscles in his eyes and therefore the last vestiges of communication – he was truly 'locked in'. I ceased to wheel him in his chair to sit in front of the computer since he could not operate it at all. A few days later his breathing became very shallow. He had always enjoyed going into the country so one morning I suggested we go to a small local nature reserve; he could not respond but I sensed his agreement. I could not take him into the reserve because entry is via a stile but there is a small farm road just outside the fence and I wheeled him along that. It was intensely peaceful with no sounds other than those of nature. At the top of the lane I turned the wheelchair round so that Philip could look down the length of the reserve to the hills beyond. My heart was full to bursting with the need to share with Philip all that I was feeling. Eventually I said 'My darling, I think you are leaving me'. Though he had no way to respond, I had a strong sense of his relief and perhaps, even, release. There were many tears as I talked some more and we shared the stillness for about an hour. The following morning his three children came from different parts of the country and after they had gone that afternoon, as I held him and talked to him, his breathing finally stopped.

Philip was never satisfied that he had completed his writing and all that he wanted to communicate; had he lived longer, I am sure that he would still be revising and expanding the work. But now he is gone and this book is his memorial. Through much self-criticism, it tells of a life lived well and courageously, with grace and with hope.

Gabrielle Grace
July 2011

ADVENTURE'S RESTING PLACE

Through rolling hills and
Gentle watered meadowlands
We wend our way to church.
Quiet this serried place today,
This holy, often noisy space:
And quieted our hearts before
The empty space of death
Disguised in unobtrusive,
Lilied, wreaths of love.

What good is this, this slow
Determined dance of neuro-
Disconnection? A fertile mind,
A restless spirit and a
Generous heart imprisoned, yet let
Loose to dance another tempo,
Hum another tune, and ride
A wilder storm, while held in
Love and friendship's firm embrace.

In Eucharist we give our thanks
And for a friend now gone
Make anamnesis: what courage
We recall, what mystery we explore in
Incensed air of loss and
Inner dereliction! And yet what hidden,
Subtle joy, what reckless hope
Awaits in bread and wine, and in
Pain's broken circle re-connected?

Edgar Ruddock, July 2010

*On returning from the funeral of Philip, friend, priest, pioneer and
adventurer, who wrestled for three years with Motor Neurone Disease.*

INTRODUCTION

When you are dying, there are things you want to say – often things you should have said years before. There are things you want to do before it becomes impossible. There are memories you want to share and people and places you hope to see once more. And some questions become much more important than before.

It starts with the personal. Why me? How long have I got? And it then broadens. How will my wife, Gaby, cope with both her changed life and my unexpected death? Then even broader. Who is in control of life? Have I been too occupied with myself and not with issues affecting millions round the world – not just disasters like the 2004 tsunami and the Haiti earthquake, but millions day-by-day? How should the Church deal with these big issues? The whole process made me look at what was important to me in my personal faith. If I had known that I would soon die, would that have changed anything?

In July 2007 I was given a terminal diagnosis – Motor Neurone Disease. Life changed physically, emotionally and practically. As my body deteriorated, it made me reflect more on what life was for and how it should be lived – particularly what interventions should be allowed at the beginning and end of life and who should be able to decide.

I spend my time lying in bed or sitting in a wheelchair at the computer, using my eyes to work an on-screen keyboard. I am very lucky to have this – the last in a long series of technical devices. But each new device indicates a further deterioration. It makes me wonder how much more can I cope with; will my life cease to be real? And what has God to do with it all?

One way I have coped with it all has been through exploring Christian beliefs and teachings as well as reflecting on my own life. Writing this has occupied my time and given me one thing to look forward to (no doubt a psychiatrist would have a field day with that). In the material chosen I distinguish pain from suffering and look at suffering from personal and biblical viewpoints. Then there is a look at my personal history and how this has affected my beliefs: while my illness has obviously made me think more about the end of life, I was surprised by much else that emerged. I go on to think through two big issues important to people with terminal diseases – assisted suicide and human embryology. Then, some conclusions.

In many ways my life had already been changed through visits made overseas as part of my three jobs over my last twenty-two working years. I was privileged to meet so many people in developing countries. They were often living in conditions, both physical and social, which amazed and horrified me. Amazed by hospitality which often cost them huge amounts of personal resources; singing, dancing and laughing; and above all the close communities and families we could all learn from. Horrified by the effects of corrupt national leadership and the greed of 'developed' countries. Despite all this, the vast majority of those I met had deep faith.

In many such countries I would not have survived this far, despite family support. Few countries could meet the continuing cost of keeping me alive, and some cultures would see MND as a mental disease, damaging to the family's likelihood of a decent marriage for their children. I would be hidden away. Despite this, I doubt a believer with my condition would change or question their faith; they live in a world where faith is totally integrated into the whole of their lives. To put all this in perspective (but not to gain sympathy) I need to go through my present-day reality – physical, emotional and practical. This is dealt with in Chapter 1 and in some parts may not be pleasant to read.

Philip Wetherell
Wellington
Somerset
2010

CHAPTER 1

Sean Connery, Islamist or the Messiah?

When my beard and hair were very short people would say 'Sean Connery, pleased to meet you,' or something similar. It was often outside pubs or passing on the street, but my 'carers' saw the resemblance too – at least to begin with. Sometimes I was taken for an Islamist, partly because I wore a beard without a moustache. For seven years I caught a bus each working day across south London to Brixton. If I had a suntan, a longer beard and particularly if I was wearing my Afghan hat, I would find an empty seat next to me. This was especially true after the London bombing. Now, 'Lo, he comes with clouds descending' is frequently sung by visitors to our home as I descend to the ground floor in my through-floor lift. It was mildly amusing the first few times but after that it became difficult since it is physically impossible for me to force a smile to show pretence at amusement. So, I am not Sean Connery, or an Islamist or the Messiah.

Am I daft, deaf and over-emotional? Yes: I admit one but, as many disabled people discover, some people assume I am all three. Patronising loud voices are common and I have become used to slow, simple words. Because I cannot speak, many assume I am also deaf. I am certainly much more emotional than before but, as described below, I have little control over how that manifests itself.

So, who am I? I know my body has changed, but what else has happened? I look later at faith issues – for now it is physical, emotional and practical changes.

Physical

Physically, things changed rapidly. Three months before diagnosis I thought I had a problem with muscle cramp or a trapped nerve. Three months after diagnosis I could hardly walk, six months after I was in a wheelchair, nine months after I lost the ability to speak, a year after diagnosis I lost the use of both hands and the ability to swallow food. Now I am totally paralysed from the neck down and this is how it is for me - I am totally physically reliant on other people.

Each day begins with my wife, Gaby, giving me medication and food direct into my stomach through a tube usually called a 'PEG'. Professional carers then arrive and hoist me out of bed, shower and dress me and put me in a wheelchair. I then have a bag attached to the back of the chair with a pump which puts more food through the PEG system. A few hours later the whole process is reversed - I am put to bed and rest for a few hours. After that I am got up again and later put back to bed for the night. Except for getting me up six days a week and the pre-rest routine on two or three days a week, all this is done by Gaby. Each time there is at least one hoisting and medication. The whole procedure takes up about five hours of each day.

The rest of the day is mostly spent at the computer, using amazing technology which needs only the movement of my eyes to move a cursor round the screen exactly where I want. There is an on-screen keyboard, so I can 'type' by holding the cursor over a letter for just over a second. It is the only way I can communicate independently. We also have a one-to-one device called a Megabee; to use it I spell out words by looking at each letter in turn and they are registered electronically by the other person. Without these two devices I can only say 'yes' or 'no' through small movements of my eyes. I can get out of the house in our specially adapted van or in my battery-driven wheelchair, operated by Gaby. We go to church, musical events, local environmental and wildlife meetings, visit some accessible gardens, canal towpaths, bird reserves and specially designed countryside paths though, as a birdwatcher, there was the day I no longer had the strength to hold binoculars. So I do have some life but I am completely dependent on others to survive; and Gaby gives most of her life to me.

Emotional

Emotionally, our world has been turned upside down. The day of diagnosis ended with another emotional moment – that very day Gaby and I took the long-distance bus from London to our new home in Somerset where our furniture had already been for two months. It is the first place we had chosen together to live in, the place for the retirement due to me in another three years. We were dumbfounded, tearful, anxious, and ignorant of how the disease would progress. It felt as though all we had was each other. We spent hours in each other's arms. There were things we did not yet want to talk about – particularly the end.

While some things have been easier to deal with than we thought (such as writing a 'Living Will', which means I will not be resuscitated should I develop another life-threatening problem), others have been really difficult. Not being able to talk is the hardest for us both, followed by losing our bedroom, its new king-size bed replaced by a single electric hospital-style bed next to the hoist and the through-floor lift. I cry and laugh in response to people who visit, but I cannot always choose which emerges. I also cry when I hear of the death of another person – whether I know them or not. We do not have a TV, but we sometimes watch DVDs, and I cry at anything even mildly emotional. I even cry when watching wildlife programmes on BBC iPlayer; this happens especially when they show somewhere I have been or had hoped to go, or birds which I had seen overseas or were part of my 'wish-list'. But the occasion when I cried most was at a local choir performance in which Gaby had two solos.

Practical

Practically, many things became impossible. The day before diagnosis and our move to Somerset, Gaby had a farewell from her job and was due to start a new one the following month as manager of a local charity for the homeless. I had been hoping to continue my work (advising individuals on working in world development and recruiting volunteers and mission partners for overseas churches) through email and web initiatives and fortnightly visits to London to interview people. Gaby never started her job but became my full-time carer. Even with full government allowances, our income fell by 80%. Our lives changed in ways we never could have imagined – and we knew that in a physical sense things could only get worse. We did a few aspects of my job together for a while. I managed initially to do a bit of DIY, make a few changes in the garden, do some cooking and even a bit of driving for a couple of months. But all the domestic chores now fall to Gaby and everything is done for me.

No longer being able to speak is the obvious communication problem, but there are many others which are not so obvious. For example, I can no longer sign anything or use the Internet to buy gifts. I cannot even communicate about pain or actions which cause me discomfort. I often appear negative when I mean to be positive and vice versa. I simply react and cannot choose how I am seen or understood. I cannot close or open my eyes or mouth as I choose; at night I wear a soft eye mask – the kind worn on aeroplanes – but even that has to be put on and taken off for me. It is almost impossible to think how I or anyone else could cope in this state without a loving spouse or other carer with a close relationship.

Am I Really Me?

In so many ways I am not 'me' any more. We chose to move to Somerset so that Gaby and I could both work for a few years while getting to know the area, chosen for is varied opportunities for walking and bird watching: the Quantocks (a wonderful discovery), Dartmoor, Exmoor and the Somerset Levels just for a start. We chose the house partly for its garden; most of which, since there are steps, I now cannot access, let alone enjoy working on.

Things are not entirely negative. We quickly discovered a vibrant local community and many interest groups, from Transition Town Wellington to the Somerset Wildlife Trust, musical societies and church groups concerned with overseas development; Gaby takes me to some of them but I can make no contribution. I enjoy some radio programmes which I would not hear if I was working; DVDs, which we certainly did not bother with before; visitors, especially when they make Gaby laugh; and having Gaby around far more than would have been the case if we were both still working – all these are positive. In addition, Gaby and I have been incredibly well-supported, especially in the earlier stages of my disease. There were regular visits from physiotherapists, speech and language and occupational therapists and an array of palliative carers, district and disability nurses; plus clinic, hospice and hospital support from respiratory, neurological, orthotic and dietary specialists. We are very fortunate to live in a developed country which has free health care. The Motor Neurone Disease Association (MNDA) has also been very supportive, and bought me a swivel seat for the passenger seat of the car, so that for a few months I was able sit next to Gaby. Another charity helped me initially to cope with weakening hands as I used my computer. There was the odd bureaucratic frustration as the system worked slowly, but letters to councilors, our MP and bishop helped speed things up; decisions take a while when quite large sums of public money are being requested. We were certainly pleased with the outcome, which gave me a through-floor lift, a wet-room – which meant I could shower safely – and a path to the back gate, as it is impossible for the wheelchair to get down our front steps. Overwhelmingly, love and duty of care have been our experience.

But the disappointments listed earlier are just symbolic of the real change: I do not feel I make any contribution even to my own life, let alone the lives of others. I do not feel I am 'depressed'; rather 'patient'. I have no idea how long I will last. We know that MND is unpredictable and we have been told that mine is 'progressing rapidly'. Sometimes I feel I am just waiting for the end, and have little thought for the future. I do not think forward at all; not to next spring for the flowering of bulbs that Gaby has recently planted. I am unable to contribute to anything except through what I am now writing, so this has enormous importance to me – physically, emotionally and practically.

But why does something like this happen? I do not mean why to me, or why this specific illness, and certainly not a combination of the two. My father faced the issue about fifty years ago when he was approaching death from an entirely different physical illness. He was told by his surgeon that in twenty years his diseased organs could be replaced and the prediction was correct. Maybe in another twenty years there will be a cure for Motor Neurone Disease, especially if human embryology and associated research is allowed (Christians have differing views on this, as explored in Chapter 11). Meanwhile the questions remain: how or why do we suffer; what is true suffering; and what connections are there with faith in a loving God?

CHAPTER 2

Pain or Suffering?

Pain is necessary; suffering is not. That may not be a common understanding. In the minds of many people the two words are used simply as alternatives or they might say that 'suffering' is long-term and 'pain' shorter – perhaps sudden or the result of an accident; more acute but more treatable. Dictionary definitions seem to suggest the same overlap:

> *Pain, n. Suffering, distress, of body or mind.*

> *Suffer, v.t. & t. Undergo, experience, be subjected to, (pain, loss, grief, etc.); whence Suffering, n.[1]*

But pain is essential. If you did not receive pain from burning your finger when you accidentally touched something hot, you would end up with unusable hands. Similarly, if you got no pain from bending over too much while gardening, you might create long-term back problems. Pain is useful, if not vital, in giving us warnings about danger. Leprosy, thankfully now curable, is an example of how awful lives can be if that system – which the body relies on – fails. People suffer frightening disability, particularly in their limbs and especially their hands, because they lose the necessary feeling. So pain is needed to protect ourselves from harm.

---

[1] Concise Oxford English Dictionary, OUP Oxford; 11th Revised edition, 22 Jun 2006

Some Christians inflict pain on themselves as part of their own Good Friday, in recognition of what Jesus experienced. I remember seeing people on their bare knees climbing many steps up to a church which housed relics; they believed that if they prayed before the relics, having inflicted pain on themselves, they would have their prayers answered.

Other individual examples are well known. One of the most famous is King Henry II, who killed Thomas à Becket by leading his friends to believe that he wished to see Becket assassinated; but when he heard the news of Becket's death he walked from London to Canterbury, as instructed by the Pope, and then allowed himself to be publically punished by the monastic community. I have increasing pain, but it is self-inflicted because though I cannot shift my position, I choose to sit working at the computer – thereby inflicting pain upon my bottom.

But what about long-term suffering? It is not always purely physical; indeed it may be psychological, the result of bereavement or the kind of situation I find myself in. Suffering can include pain, particularly if it is serious and long-term, but it is a far more complicated issue than just physical pain. I am not suggesting that ongoing physical pain is easier to live with than relatively painless emotional suffering, but suffering is much broader and affects different people, including relatives of the sufferer, in different ways.

Some Christians find that suffering somehow strengthens their faith (this is looked at in Chapter 10 on Assisted Suicide) but none would wish it on others. But there are difficult questions for people of faith. Where is God in all this? Is suffering some kind of test? Is God allowing us to suffer? Does he not love us enough?

Because most of my work experience has been to do with the developing world, questions to do with God's love have particular relevance. India always comes first to mind. I was visiting a church re-building project. Women were bringing bricks, carried on their heads. They were dusty and tired, but the church was at least giving some income to those who lived over its back wall. This was a sandy area just above sea-level, frequently flooded and crammed with tiny huts built from rubbish collected from streets and from the beach. In other parts of India, as in the rest of the world, this beach would be a glorious tourist destination. Here, it was covered in human excrement, with groups using collected wood to cook what little food they had. There was no other place for either activity. What stays in my mind is the image of a tiny thin woman pushing her even more skeletal baby towards me, begging me to take him or her away, as she could no longer afford food.

I had a more distant view of a different but unfortunately too common tragedy. Again visiting a church, but this time in Rio de Janeiro, Brazil, I saw the result of a major housing disaster. Rio is a beautiful city, partly because of its beaches but, to my mind, mostly in its steep forested hills. But on the hills close to the city centre the poor build their shacks, often with no foundations, simply attached to or leaning on the one next door. On the hill I was looking at there was a muddy scar. Heavy rain had flooded down, the houses had tumbled, and unknown scores of people had been killed.

Different stories of suffering. We can blame the situation in India and Brazil (both now major developing economies) and in much of Africa on governments or international systems which allow the rich to exploit the poor, but why does our loving God allow it? Maybe the faith of Christians living in these situations is driven simply by hope for their future in another world and that is how they cope with poverty, early death, disease and exploitation by their own leaders, by overseas companies and by governments. Is it just a vain hope which helps them to get through their meagre everyday lives – that if they sustain their faith under such circumstances they will go to heaven? That may be so; but for ten years I attended a church in south east London which was ninety percent black, mostly people from west Africa; were they there because of that same hope for the future? In all our major cities African immigrants and subsequent generations have boosted declining congregations and founded many new churches.

I have been thinking through all this from both the personal and the Biblical angles but firstly, a quick diversion.

Judas Iscariot and Margaret Thatcher?

The New Testament accounts of Judas and of his death are not identical. In the Acts of the Apostles (Acts 1:18-19) he is in the field he bought with the thirty pieces of silver when suddenly he has a gruesome death (presumably punished by God) and descends into hell where he is still suffering eternal damnation. A myth I once heard suggests that he met Jesus – who, according to our Creed, spent the period between his death and Resurrection in hell – there. The only gospel to mention Judas' death is Matthew (Matthew 27:3-10) and he has a very different account. Judas is portrayed as so full of remorse for betraying Jesus that he takes his own life, though suicide is traditionally seen as defying God's will – even in my days working in parishes, burials of suicides were not allowed at many Christian cemeteries unless a diagnosis of mental illness was given. Despite these different accounts of his death,

Judas is generally seen as the most evil person in the whole of scripture. How could anyone spend all that time with such a remarkable, unique person as Jesus and betray him? The thirty pieces of silver are a powerful symbol for many of us.

There are two mysteries around Judas' betrayal. Firstly, Jesus knew it would happen, and even told a disciple – who did not do anything to stop Judas. Jesus knew he had to die. Judas, according to St. John, has a portion of bread given to him by Jesus and suddenly Satan takes over. Did Jesus have a part to play in Satan entering Judas? This would change the whole story. While Judas may have been fiddling the expenses, Jesus could surely have dealt with that, as he did with so many other sinners. However, if Jesus was indirectly responsible for Judas' death, does this have parallels with the present-day issue which many Christians struggle with – assisted suicide (see Chapter 10)?

The second mystery: why did the authorities need Judas anyway? If Jesus was such a threat, they would be aware of his identity. Judas would only be needed if they were worried about the reaction of Jesus' supporters. This is questionable since the following day they managed to persuade people to cry out for Barabbas.

How does this diversion relate to pain or suffering? Judas was a catalyst and was personally responsible for the suffering of a totally innocent man – though maybe we should describe it as 'pain' rather than 'suffering'. It was only about eighteen hours from Jesus' arrest to his death; at some time he was tortured and his nailing was dreadful, but compared with the prolonged water-boarding and electrical torture of the present day he may have been lucky.

What if Jesus had died a natural death? The core of Christianity would be lost; there might be a few followers of his ethical stance, but the movement might not have lasted beyond the generation which had known him.

So where does Margaret Thatcher come in? The UK is the third most unequal country in the developed world, in terms of the income-gap between rich and poor. Research shows that greater inequality goes hand in hand with more social problems – marriage breakdown, crime, escalating prison population, drug abuse etc. The statistics are best presented in The Spirit Level.[2] While increases in inequality have taken place under all recent UK governments (including the thirteen years of Labour Party rule which ended in 2010) the most rapid change took place during the Conservative years under Margaret Thatcher. The 'trickle down' theory never worked – the rich simply got richer.

So while Judas caused severe physical pain, the Thatcher government was responsible for our huge social problems - suffering on a vast scale.

Severe pain is difficult to cope with particularly if it becomes protracted (I am not sure I could cope with that – see Chapter 10, Assisted Suicide). But suffering has other contexts and the next chapter deals with where I am.

---

[2] Richard Wilkinson and Kate Pickett (2009) The Spirit Level, Allen Lane

CHAPTER 3

Suffering – the Reality

The two events described in this chapter took place nine months after diagnosis. I could then still use my left hand to eat and type, though very slowly. Given the rate of deterioration, I had not expected still to be alive when looking at this some sixteen months later but mentally things have not changed.

Maundy Thursday

The traditional Anglo-Catholic Maundy Thursday service gives plenty of space for thought – from the reading of the origin of the Passover (an amazing account any present-day writer would be proud of), to the dramatic story of the Last Supper and the arrest and trial of Jesus. The liturgy can include theatrical once-a-year reminders – foot-washing, the stripping of the altar, darkening of the church and then time of silence before the Reserved Sacrament surrounded by candles and flowers.

So, for this person who is uncertain of the meaning and outcome of the 'Passion' 2000 years ago (see Chapter 6, 'Selfish Salvation' for an exploration of that) what was the point of half an hour's silence in a church in 2008? For me, prayer is not a time to be asking God to change things; it is helpful only because it gives time to think deep thoughts which should lead to change through action. If that is what prayer time is for, what was going on for me that Maundy Thursday?

Because Gaby was alongside me I thought of her and all that she does for me, being so much more than just a full-time carer. That week I had managed for the last time to mix some flour and butter in a bowl on my lap, but that pastry mix was the only physical contribution I had made to our joint lives for many weeks. For the tart-maker in our household, this was now another thing to add to the list of impossibles. I was also thinking about much earlier failures – two previous marriages and bits of work I had not done well. Later Gaby reminded me of the sermon we had heard that evening about Jesus' command to love. It had made her reflect on how difficult that must be for me as I have few practical ways of sharing love beyond using the Internet to buy such things as flowers for Valentine's Day.

Half-empty or half-full?

My thoughts during that time of silence did not dwell only on the past but connected also to the future – a kind of 'glass half empty or half full' question. Am I pleased to have survived long enough to see the daffodils along the streets of Wellington that help to win it regional 'in bloom' competitions, or overjoyed to see the first migrant sand martins? Or am I thinking 'that's the last time I'll see them and what's the point; just another day of frustration and loss of energy'? I found myself veering towards the latter. Somehow it would be different if I were 99 years old; yes, I could live to be 100 or even more and, while the chances of survival might not be more than mine actually are now, I would then be on the 'half full' side.

My thoughts (rather than simply my mood) have partly to do with external changes. Perhaps oddly to those who have not experienced something as degenerative as MND, it is new equipment that is sometimes the hardest to take. Some of this has to do with the fact that it rarely does all that was hoped – maybe a month ago the gadget would have been OK, but now it does not achieve what we really need. It all contributes to the glass being half empty. Whatever device comes (the latest around that time was a device to help me sit up in bed, I think the sixtieth of assorted bits and pieces, some now sent back) it is a symbol of decline, further weakness and a closer end to some function.

The classic was the night-time breathing machine which produced air in response to my own intake of breath or, particularly important, when my breathing slowed or got weaker. It worked through a mask to be worn in bed. We both hated it; the noise it made, the cold air, the leaks that made my eyes water, and the end of any cuddling in bed (already limited by immobility). Because it did not seem to respond to my breathing as it got shallower as I drifted off to sleep, we took it back to the hospital and the settings were modified. But we chose not to bring the machine back home, not for any of the given reasons (though we spoke of them all) but because behind it all was too big a reality. When breathing goes, so does life – and we do not want to think of my life simply being kept going by a machine.

Soon my daytime breathing became weaker. Sitting around, listening to anything which was not exciting, even working at the computer if it did not require some active thinking, meant I nodded off. Any exertion at all, even assisted standing up (then still just possible) made my face go red and hot. The promised headaches came too – because at night, without the machine, there were periods when my breathing came and went. Returning the machine was daft, but I still do not want to accept that I now need it.

Losing who you are?

On Easter Day 2008 I could still just make myself understood, and Gaby and I spoke about some deeply personal matters, but the link to any Easter message was, if anything, very tenuous. Easter is about new beginnings, new relationships, hope in the future. Our very tearful discussion was about losing who I am (equally painful to both of us) and realising how important the things we did together, which were now impossible, had been in our relationship. Soon we would have to abandon our double bed as I would need a special electric bed. Carers would be needed to help with washing and dressing. Mechanical devices, such as a hoist to transfer from bed to commode or wheelchair, would be needed too. In all the ways that relationships are formed and sustained we were losing out. Worst by far is not being able to talk. All that I can now manage is a very slow response to practical questions, though limited sign language is usually more accurately understood. (Things have got much worse since writing this – the electric bed, hoist, daily carers, a special computer and other communication aids have all helped but all of them are signs of physical deterioration).

At times there is physical pain as my muscles weaken. Stiff joints seem to be a permanent feature of life, only improved a little by medication. But the emotional suffering is harder and made worse by something physical – the inability to cry or laugh without sounding like a braying donkey and with a much distorted face. Often I cannot make myself do one rather than the other – I laugh when I should cry and vice versa. Another inability to relate.

The words of John Austin, from the group of severely disabled people described in Chapter 4, are more positive than mine, perhaps because of their greater underlying faith:

> *We are learning what it could mean to receive what God offers us to live creatively within our reality; learning what it is to be laid bare, stripped of roles, responsibilities, masks and dignity; learning the presence and providence of God within the sense of the absence of God; learning that the pain bearers continue to take their place within the redemptive process; and learning that the Church speaks much of pain and suffering but is embarrassed by it.* [1]

It is obviously helpful to see God giving us the ability to deal with all this, and I am in admiration of a group of individuals who endure so much long-term suffering. I agree that it is helpful to live creatively, if only by sorting out relationships, papers and other possessions – in my case sending my thesis archive material to an Oxford University library and sorting family material with my children.

Six months after diagnosis my watch strap broke. I have not replaced it and I do not wear a watch any more. The diary that used to be central to working life is unused in a drawer. Use of time is not dictated by me but by assessment visits, clinic and hospital appointments and carers. But in another way 'time' is a very different issue - it is about dealing with change.

Gaby has said that it feels as if she is already 'losing' me – the 'me' she worked alongside for nearly twelve years before we fell in love and married. We shared so many things: politics and travel, music and cooking, walking and bird-watching. I let

---

[1] John Austin, Church Times, 03/03/2006

her down when it came to dancing, which she loves, but we were together in so much. The 'me' she had known is no longer there and, apart from writing 'thank you' in my daily computer notes, there is little I can now do for her. A sideways nestling of my head against hers is about all I can do to show affection. I understand her anguish that I can no longer 'give' anything or be involved in any real way in our everyday life together.

A 'Quiet Day'

About ten days before that Maundy Thursday we had been at another traditional event for that time of the year – a Lenten 'Quiet Day'. The two talks we attended were on the subject of 'fear'. After the first there was a questionnaire on fear designed to help us think it through: 'Are you willing to explore your fears?' We were then asked to consider different kinds of fear, whether it can ever be useful and what our relationship was with our fear. There were many other detailed questions and lists we could check out, but 'your relationship with fear' and 'what's the worst thing that could happen to you?' were those I needed to address.

My relationship with fear? My real fear gets stronger as I can do less and particularly when I can relate less. I am not too fearful of physical pain because, in my case so far, there has always been a solution to that. At the moment choking is not a major concern – food goes directly into my stomach and excess saliva, which can make me choke, is controlled by drugs. Neither am I fearful about the physical aspects of dying – I am sure the local hospice can advise or deal with that. It is not the physical that is frightening.

So what is the worst thing that could happen? The answer to that second question is one thing which has not changed – it is now, and would always have been, the loss of Gaby. That is unchanged in a personal, emotional sense, but losing her would now be even harder as I rely on her in so many practical ways. Living with no real close relationship while having a progressive disease like mine has to be the worst thing that could happen.

I heard only a part of a radio report about a man with MND who had gone to Switzerland to be permitted a lawful suicide. As I understood it, he had to be 'well enough' to be able to take personal responsibility for the deed and the description given of his condition at that time did not sound much worse than mine. He had relatives but, as I understood it, no partner. I understand why he felt that was the right thing to do (this is looked at in detail in Chapter 10, Assisted Suicide).

The next worst thing has to be the inability to communicate. I have some wonderful devices but they all require movement, which is already getting harder. But even now there are some communication problems which can be both annoying and frustrating. People often think I am angry when they are helping me because my grunting is misunderstood. I make a hideous noise when yawning which can be frightening or make people think I am mentally challenged. Children find my vacant stare a little frightening. Kissing is impossible as my lips have almost no muscle power and get caught in my teeth – I need hugs to make me know that at least the nerve endings in my body still work. I now have wonderful 'carers' from an agency helping me to get up in the morning and who treat me as a mentally-competent adult. Others are different. The nurse who was asked to be quieter because my hearing has become more acute joked about it very loudly and annoyed me far more than non-medical people who, seeing this silent man slumped in a wheelchair with open mouth and staring eyes, assume I am deaf and stupid.

'Real' suffering

The externals may seem petty, but the real suffering is in not being able to be who I want to be in my relationships with other people, particularly with Gaby, and my related fear is that I do not see a way that can change. As everything else slows down, so will my ability to relate.

Of less importance – though not insignificant – is that my relationship with the wider world has almost broken down. Apart from two medical appointments I had not been out of the house that week in Lent. There were little moments – like discovering that we may have a blackbird nesting in the back garden – but more generally, how can I enjoy things in the community that I can no longer be part of, or the things which have always been my interests? I spend 90% of my waking time at the computer, mostly doing this writing. The small bits of work I am still doing will soon be given up, so what will happen to my days then? Will I be of value to anyone, including myself?

That has all sounded both miserable and negative. As I already mentioned, there are many positive stories from people further along the progression of MND than I am – the MND Association website is full of them. Not one story mentions any faith element – of looking forward to meeting Jesus. Is it that they are psychologically different, or are they hiding their real fears? Perhaps the Association wants only positive stories.

Or might I change? With an electric wheelchair, warmer weather coming, the garden starting to look nice, the blackbirds and a chance to get out and about more, will I have less fear? Does small-scale enjoyment placate larger-scale fears? Small things can certainly help; the best for me so far being the five-year-old daughter of some visiting friends. With the clarity and logic of her conversation she made me laugh in a way I had not done for months. Maybe that was because to her I was just a man sitting in a funny chair who made occasional weird noises, so she remained herself rather than having to make any concession to me.

I was previously able to look up MND on websites, and the one I remember is the story of a man diagnosed at 27 who lived for five years. The written diary was bearable, though his stories of increasing disability, sleeping and breathing problems were not easy to read. The difficult bit was the attached video. What made me moan, in a crying rather than laughing mode, was the child born since his diagnosis climbing onto a settee and then leaning over onto the wheelchair to give him a kiss. But what made me turn it off was the unbearable picture of him with his wife – his face distorted like mine as they hugged and cried. Their relationship was still alive, as mine is for me, but it is so difficult to show it and express it in a practical and supportive sense. I may be told that it doesn't matter that my contribution is not the same as it was but, however many times I am told, that does not seem to affect how I feel. Mentally I am not a vegetable, but my inability to fully contribute to relationships is my biggest concern and fear for the future.

When I get to the point of almost total inactivity and I am unable to communicate in any way, I may not care too much if a particular night is my last. I have already signed my Living Will, and I hope that will be sufficient protection from becoming a vegetable. I know Gaby wants me around for as long as is possible and there are a few things I want to do – mainly sorting out where some of my possessions should go, and writing some 'final' letters. I have no list of people or places to see. The odd outing we manage can be very enjoyable, not least just feeling the wind and the rain, but it usually leaves me feeling frustrated, thinking what I would have been able to do if I could walk and talk. In the end I don't think I will be the person who will decide when and how I die but, to return to the theme of this chapter, I am not sure how I will cope with the suffering – both mental and physical.

The worst thing

Only one of the many professional people who has visited, listened to and advised us has asked me, 'How are you feeling inside?' She works for the local hospice, so is perhaps more aware of the need for such questions to be broached. The other, equally good, professionals do not deal all the time with terminally-ill people so maybe they find it too hard, or it is against their professional rules. I could not cope with being probed all the time anyway, especially in the carers' cheery 'How are you today?' kind of way. The answer to her question was that I feel worst when I think about how Gaby will cope when I am not here. She has acquired a huge number of practical skills in the last few months and is very organised and efficient; but when the purpose of all the love that fills her life disappears and I am not physically here to be part of the partnership we had planned in this place, then what will life be for her?

That is my greatest regret, my fundamental fear and strongest emotion. Every time Gaby comes into the bedroom after my afternoon rest I have a brief emotional sob as an automatic reaction. These feelings are much more significant to me and cause much more suffering than any physical pain.

CHAPTER 4

Suffering – the Biblical Theory

I am not sure how I would cope with severe physical pain but, for me and for many terminally ill people, other elements are more serious. The change in relationships, inability to communicate, the gradual but unpredictable decline, total reliance on provided care and above all (for me at least), the feeling that I am not really who I was, and certainty not who I wished to be. And the person who has to deal with all that and cope with massive change once I have gone is Gaby. So, what does our Christian faith have to say about all this and will it help either Gaby or me to cope?

At the core of Christian belief is the suffering of Jesus on our behalf, leading to his death and resurrection. One issue vital to many Christians historically and in the present day is how to cope with persecution in their everyday lives. Alongside that issue is one involving all of us: how do we deal with the causes of suffering and whether God is responsible? Why do we all, particularly Christians, suffer? How much has it to do with Jesus?

Jesus suffers

A selection of images of Jesus from around the world was produced by a group of Christian agencies which concentrate on working to support overseas churches[1]. Many of the

---

[1] The Christ We Share (1999), CMS, USPG, Methodist Church

pictures reflect the cultures they come from – for example, one from Korea shows Jesus carrying not a cross but what appears to be a lump of rock. Close examination shows a line across the middle and what was a rock turns into a map of the divided Korea. I used the pictures many times and I remember two particular occasions on which the question of suffering was central.

The first was a youth group in south east London, all black, mostly born in the UK, with parents mostly from West Africa. I asked them to choose the picture which meant the most to them. As children brought up in this country, and very much part of their current teenage culture, I did not expect them to choose an African image. However, neither did I expect the one they chose – it was the well-known picture of the actor Robert Powell from the film 'Jesus of Nazareth'. Jesus is portrayed looking beyond his present life with steely blue eyes. But it was the crown of thorns and bleeding forehead that made them choose this picture; they explained: 'Jesus suffered for us'.

The second occasion was at a conference for missionaries on furlough or recently returned to the UK. The charity I worked for arranged several of these gatherings each year. We used the selection of images as an 'ice-breaker'. The participants chose a wide variety of favourites, depending partly on which country they had returned from, what work they had become involved in and their theological stance.

We also asked them to choose their least favourite. Almost all stood in front of a picture of Jesus on the cross: a wooden carving of a distorted body with head bent forward; the mouth was larger than normal and obviously expressing the pain the whole naked body was experiencing – very unlike those serene faces we are used to in paintings of the Crucifixion. On that occasion one participant was a severely disabled man in a wheelchair: the others assumed he was joining them for the same reason but they had a moment of embarrassed silence when they heard him say in his distorted voice: 'This is my Jesus'.

Two very different stories; but examples of how, in different ways, Christians see the suffering of Jesus as happening on behalf of the whole human race. Because he was sinless, in some way he made it possible for believers who confess their own sin to receive salvation. For many who suffer now this can be a source of comfort. The Bible says that Jesus *'learned obedience in the school of suffering, and once perfected, became the source of eternal salvation for all who obey him'* (Hebrews. 5:8-9, NEB).

In the traditional Christian view at least, sin is dealt with by faith because Jesus has, by being truly human and without sin, enabled us to join him in eternal life – providing we have the correct faith and have confessed all our sins. To that basic understanding is added a variety of beliefs by denominations or individuals. Some Christians attribute individual suffering to sin – punishment in prison, or earlier death due to misuse of drugs and poor diet, for example. But the millions of innocent poor, for what reason do they suffer, and is it enough to say they will be rewarded in heaven?

Persecution A: our experience

Suffering can sometimes result from religious choices and divisions; for example, inter-faith conflict (between Muslims and Christians in places such as northern Nigeria); converting to a different faith (in parts of India this means moving to a different village); or even divisions within the same faith (such as between Sunni and Shia Muslims, resulting in car bombings in places like Iraq).

Within our faith, Christians are no different: we have been at war, we have had the Inquisition inflicted on us, and people in the UK once had to change denomination according to the will of the monarch (or Cromwell). Recent years have seen a surprising alliance between Roman Catholics and Evangelicals – both opposed to abortion, gay rights and the role of women in ministry. This may appear to be discrimination rather than serious suffering; but imagine a lesbian woman with a vocation to become priest or minister, whether or not she favours abortion. She will feel let down by her church and possibly by God. Suffering is not just physical.

Close to my vicarage in Southampton was a church building with no visible windows. Individuals and families were converting to a sect based solely in that church. Members were not allowed social contact outside their own sect. Some Jehovah's Witnesses behave similarly, severing contact with the rest of their families. Women who convert to strict forms of Islam have similar restrictions placed upon them and conversion out of Islam can result in complete family cut-off. Religious groups so certain of their own angle on doctrine can make believers' families suffer by causing them to be shunned as people liable to corrupt the truth.

Persecution B: the Biblical view

Conversion from Judaism to the new Christian faith in New Testament times – often at that time a family decision – meant opposition from neighbours, and certainly from the religious leadership who wanted to avoid conflict with the occupying political authorities. Such opposition, if not persecution, was experienced because of the change, the leaving of one culture to join another. It is easy to see why comparisons with the suffering of Jesus were used to demonstrate faithfulness and even the certainty of eternal life.

In the New Testament Christians are warned of persecution. True salvation is about following Jesus: *'When you have behaved well and suffer for it, your fortitude is a fine thing in the sight of God'* (1 Peter 2:20, NEB). In Matthew 5:1, Jesus teaches that those who suffer insults and persecution for his sake should accept it as there will be a rich reward in heaven. That discourse finishes with the story of building on sand or rock. The one who hears the word and rejects it is the builder on sand: like the house, he falls with a great crash (Matthew 7:27). However, all of these texts relate to behaviour, faith and the future – not to present suffering.

Scripture has different explanations for suffering. Do we suffer because we are sinful; is God testing us? Is it punishment or is our knowledge of medicine and psychology now so advanced that today such questions are irrelevant?

A matter of sin?

My second marriage collapsed and, though I continued preaching, I did not seek to regain permission to celebrate the Eucharist. The Church of England acted correctly once the divorce was finalised. With pastoral care I had not expected, I was taken though a legal process which meant a five year minimum ban from priestly functions. At the end of that time my vicar negotiated with our bishop for 'permission to officiate' (PTO) and gave me, as my first Eucharistic celebration, the most important service in the Christian year – the Easter service. In early May that same year I first noticed

41

signs of what was diagnosed three months later as Motor Neurone Disease. Was God punishing me for even daring to think I was worthy of handling what the Church believes is his body and blood?

We hear daily in the news of natural disasters, wars, rape, children forced to join militia, violence and outbreaks of deadly disease which usually affect the poorest. But in New Testament times life was even harder than in the poorest countries today. One estimate suggests that then the majority of children died before the age of five and perhaps as many as one in four women died in childbirth. The causes of illness were not certain and treatment often not possible. Jesus was confronted by many who wanted healing and he shared the accepted belief that much sickness had to do with sin.

In Matthew's Gospel we hear of the man who was *'dumb and possessed by a devil'* (Matthew. 9:32, NEB) where there seems to be a link between possession and physical illness: *'the devil was cast out and the patient recovered his speech'* (Matthew. 9:33, NEB). Another story appears to separate a man's suffering of paralysis from sin; Jesus responds to criticism of his forgiving of sin with *'Is it easier to say 'Your sins are forgiven' or to say 'Stand up and walk?''* – which Jesus then commands him to do. But forgiveness and healing are presented in sequence, and the first may be necessary for the second to happen (Matthew. 9:2-8, NEB). So why do we suffer? And why does any particular person suffer? And me; why me?

Suffering as a sign of faith?

For many of us it seems that suffering is absolutely essential to the character-building process, and it is only through suffering that those called by God can learn what is required to gain salvation. This is because Christ's own suffering perfected him, matured him and made him complete. This belief may be based on, and is certainly backed up by, Old Testament passages such as Psalm 119:71, in which the writer suggests, 'How good it is for me to have been punished, to school me in thy statutes' (NEB). A traditional interpretation would be that while suffering in no way *feels* good, it is good in terms of results, and is therefore necessary. For some people, one outcome of suffering is that they feel they mature in their faith. There are many wonderful stories told by long-term sufferers and victims about how they have grown; how their understanding has changed or a new role has been discovered.[1] Should we deduce from that the idea that our faith is somehow imperfect if we are not coping with suffering, or that God is not allowing us to suffer since we are not strong enough in faith?

To test our faith?

The best-known story on the theme of testing faith is the Old Testament book of Job, where the good man loses everything, and is told by family and friends to curse God for what is happening to him – and he refuses, despite being tested and made to suffer. Job felt that God was working directly in his life, and nothing could prevent that or change the way it happened. If the same is true for us, we may have to look forward to a lifetime of overcoming a variety of challenges,

---

[1] Donald Eadie (1999) Grain in Winter, Epworth Press; Philip Simmons (2002) Learning to Fall, Hodder and Stoughton

which will lead to character development and spiritual growth.

Some Muslims appear to support that view. In a BBC Thought for the Day, reflecting on an earthquake in China, Professor Mona Siddiqui said:

> *As one Islamic scholar puts it, "Suffering is the point where the perpetual contradictions of our existence intersect: our knowledge that we are free, our knowledge that we are not; our knowledge that we are masters and creators, and our knowledge that we are frail and transitory beings." Indeed the Qur'an itself is candid and clear that we will all be tested in different ways: "We have indeed created man into a life of pain, toil and trial, and most certainly we shall try you by means of fear, hunger and loss of worldly goods." We can't take God's trials as the defining aspect of our relationship with him, but nor can we dismiss them as the fundamental mystery of a benign world order. The question for ordinary believers is a double edged one - what does God gain by testing us and what do we gain by being tested?* [2]

She continues by answering these questions:

> *For some, suffering results in a loss of belief. God is seen as an arbitrary being who causes pain without caring. For others, there is refuge only with God, for there is no life outside of God. I think that God gains nothing.*

---

[2] Prof. Mona Siddiqui, Thought for the Day, 15 April 2010, BBC

Hardship

Regardless of its cause, many would argue that hardship can lead to character development. I remember preaching under a tree in a rural area outside Mozambique's capital city. It was one of the few areas recently freed from occupation, but attacks by rebels were still possible. In the adjacent field was a government military tank. It was amazing to see such a dedicated group of all ages gathering for a Eucharist whenever a local priest could manage to get there a few times a year, and as a guest I wanted to encourage them. I said how wonderful it was to see so many young people there, whereas in the majority of the UK churches I visited there were so few. The weekly leader of the congregation, a young man chosen because he had some education, came up to me afterwards and pressed some money into my hand 'for the young people of Britain'. I discovered afterwards that this was his three-month salary, just handed over to him by the priest I had accompanied. A modern version of the widow's mite?

Hardship can help to build community and forge strong bonds. It might help people to understand and be alongside the suffering of Jesus, but I find it difficult to accept that it is *only* through suffering that we can be saved. True, in Jesus' words, the comfortably rich should give up their possessions and therefore their security, but that is because something other than love is dominating life. Human suffering is not what Jesus wants for us; it is a part of the reality of existence.

A group of severely disabled Christians from Birmingham, including ministers and nuns, meets as regularly as they can. On their behalf John Austin wrote an article for the Church Times. He suggested quite rightly that:

Theology mustn't simply be left to those who are fit and strong, and able to spend all day in the library or on the computer. Theology must also be wrestled for through pain and disability: the raw materials of our encounters with a mysterious God, whose name seems sometimes hidden. That's how Jacob got his hip dislocated. With our spinal injuries, MS or artificial joints we are well qualified to carry on the struggle. [3]

I certainly agree with the first part of that quote but, while Jacob may well have learned from his dislocated hip (Gen. 32:25), I am not taken by the possible implication of a mysterious God being responsible for suffering.

Divine Retribution

In the first chapter of the Epistle to the Romans, divine retribution is seen to fall on *'the godless wickedness of men'* (Romans 1:18, NEB). Because people have refused to honour what is apparently obvious about Jesus, who revealed God to us, we suffer. This causes the *'consequent degradation'* (1:24) of our bodies. In contrast, in chapter 8 verses 18-25, a picture is painted for us of a God who seems to have willed our difficulties: *'For the created universe waits with eager expectation for God's sons to be revealed. It was made the victim of frustration, not by its own choice, but because of him who made it so'* (Romans 8:19f, NEB). It is as if suffering were given to us in order that we should ache for something better. I find that picture totally alien to any God I would personally want to

---

[3] John Austin, Church Times, 03/03/2006, available from donaldeadie@tiscali, who can also give information about the group.

worship. Even linking it to the suffering and resurrection of God's own Son is not convincing as an argument. The idea that if God had eliminated or outlawed suffering there would be no cross and therefore no Resurrection – either for Jesus or for us – is nonsensical. Did God have to invent suffering so that he could then give us the opportunity to overcome it?

Other people with long-term illnesses have a very different take on Jesus' suffering. John Austin again:

> *...we can, at times, catch glimpses of God in pain. We examine the mystery that there are those in the world who are the 'pain-bearers'...and how sometimes some good comes out of the suffering. We keep working at the notion that somehow pain and suffering has its place in the redemptive process - work that can only be authentically tackled by those who know what they are talking about.*
>
> *For most 'able-bodied' people, this only rarely happens, and is seen as undignified or unpleasant. Can we begin to uncover theological and spiritual meaning within this experience of our bodies being made vulnerable and handled by other people? Christ at the end of his life was stripped, stretched horizontal, and handed over to others, and is shown as almost naked on the cross.*
>
> *The washing of feet and the stripping of the altars are part of the spirituality of Holy Week. For us, there is a need to connect that spirituality of physical weakness and vulnerability with our own experience of weakness.* '[4]

Personal suffering can of course help us to understand that of others – now I am in a wheelchair I understand far better the feelings people have about lack of access to many facilities. It

---

[4] John Austin, op.cit

also helps us to appreciate care and those working so hard to ameliorate the effects of suffering. Perhaps it is my lack of spirituality, but I could not accept a God who causes suffering deliberately, to create such understanding and appreciation. It is as if the serpent in the second of the Genesis creation myths was encouraged by God so that Adam and Eve would be banished from the Garden of Eden, find themselves in the 'real' world and learn to suffer. We are at least told in 1 Peter 5:10 that the suffering will be brief (that is, confined to this world); but there is no mention of its cause.

Just getting it wrong?

In 1 Corinthians 11, Paul deals with this very differently. He is writing of the new covenant, sealed by the blood of Christ which, when drunk by followers, is a memorial proclaiming the death of the Lord until he comes (verses 23-26). Anyone who eats the bread or drinks the cup unworthily is guilty of desecration, so we must test ourselves before we do that – hence the tradition I was brought up with, that if you were late to church and missed the confession you could not receive communion. Paul then identifies a cause of illness and death: *'For he who eats and drinks, eats and drinks judgement on himself if he does not discern the body. That is why many of you are feeble and sick, and a number have died'* (verses 29-30, NEB). This happens because we are under God's judgement and are disciplined to save us from being condemned as the rest of the world will be. So can illness and even death be caused by misunderstanding the real content of Holy Communion?

Is there an assumption that illness (which can result from sin if 1 Corinthians 11:29-30 is right) will also disappear with the washing away of sin? At the end of people's lives, a final confession is said to have much the same effect – you die with a clean slate. But none of this solves the problem of indiscriminate human suffering.

Dukkha – 'the general unsatisfactoriness of human life'

Examining scripture in this way helps me to work through what I believe, but there are others who have done much more work on this. I went to Peter Cotterell, whom I would describe as a fairly radical evangelical. His book Mission and Meaninglessness[5] is subtitled 'The good news in a world of suffering and disorder', and has as its central theme *dukkha*, which is used in Buddhism as one of the three characteristics of human existence. It means 'the general unsatisfactoriness of human life'. Cotterell suggests:

> *The religions of the world have at least this in common: they all believe that the human existence ought to make sense, that we ought to have meaning; and all religions offer an explanation of dukkha.* (p.7)

Life is meaningless?

It is Cotterell's final chapter which relates most to where I am now. It begins (p.261) with what seems a very negative summary:

---

[5] Peter Cotterell (1990) Mission and Meaninglessness, SPCK

It is the common experience of humanity that between the two apparent boundaries of human existence, birth and death, life is characterised by 'unsatisfactoriness', by dukkha. Life appears to be without ultimate meaning. The apparently random intrusion of disease and death, the apparently inexplicable occurrence of accident ... requires us either to accept that life is meaningless or to seek a reinterpretation of the human condition through religion or revelation.

I am not totally convinced, but that may be because of my understanding of the word 'common'. Many people, with or without faith, have 'satisfactory' relationships, enjoy much of their lives and even approach death feeling they have achieved something. Cotterell sees religion as one way in which many manage that: Hindus in poverty hope for reincarnation into a better life; Muslims see everything as willed by Allah and the response is submission. In African tradition, human problems are caused by neglect of the spirit world. In the distorted Christian belief (my adjective) called Prosperity Theology, failure and resulting poverty are due to lack of faith. Each religion offers an explanation, constructs its view of the world and requires a lifestyle to cope with it. Christianity is different from most other faiths because it is a 'missionary' religion; the life of Christ meant he was able to respond to the human condition and through him God was able to deal with *dukkha.*

I find Cotterell's two final sections the most helpful. These are on Political and Economic Oppression and The Experience of Natural Disaster. They point to human greed and mismanagement as the key to much of what happens. Natural disasters may be explained by scientific laws which can appear destructive but which also create the land on which we live. In response to such disasters, many Christians respond more than non-believers by contributing funds or even sharing people's poverty and disadvantage, to manifest God's love in the world.

The problem of individual suffering remains. One of my visits to Mozambique, when I was working for the missionary society USPG, was to further co-operation and partnership between the Portuguese-speaking parts of the Anglican Church. With a bishop from Brazil, I was visiting churches, schools and agricultural projects which it had been impossible to see during the years of revolution. One night I shared a room in a rural home with the Brazilian bishop. We each had a far-from-perfect mosquito net. We were both bitten. He had been advised that anti-malarials were not needed. He died. I took the pills and did not. Bad advice, and just one innocent victim joining the millions who die each year from similar lack of protection – though mostly because they cannot afford it.

Cotterell also deals with disease and death, and questions those who interpret the fact that they are not suffering as part of their 'success', and as an indicator of their worthiness of heaven. Followers of Prosperity Theology seek material success – God rewards those who have been good and hold the true faith. Cotterell then quotes one exponent who believes that true Christians have been redeemed from all bad things, whether sickness, financial problems or spiritual need (p.269). True Christians do not die of disease, but of 'old age'. Cotterell's biblical answer is that it is safer to lose one's life than to succeed in it (based on Jn. 12:25). It is similarly better not to be rich, as the first shall be last and the last shall be first.

...this is the Christian response to the dukkha of illness and death. That God may well heal miraculously. Of course it

may be so. But that in our illness we are sharing in the common experience of peoples everywhere, and at that cost we are earning the right to say to the peoples around us that we understand. Just as God understands because he, too, once came among us and experienced not merely death, but death on the cross. (p.272)

Cotterell then points out that even in old age, it is generally a disease or trauma that brings an end to life and it is easy to find biblical lists of sins, putting a guilt load on any Christian who gets sick. There is no evidence that faithfulness brings treasure on earth, even for those who believe in treasure awaiting them beyond death.

Cotterell does however believe that healing takes place as a result of prayer. I am sure that evidence of the power of prayer is available but to my mind there are usually other explanations; for instance, statistics show that hospital patients who have happy homes to go back to recover more quickly than those who do not. I cannot believe that some people, whether or not they have deep faith, remain ill because not enough prayer is said, or that the all-knowing God needs a nudge to get someone out of pain. Why should God choose to answer some prayers and not others, or ignore the immense suffering of the poor across the world while so many are praying that it will end?

Putting Cotterell's insights together with my own look at biblical material, the New Testament image of suffering might be summarised as follows. It happens at the end of time, or with death, for those who have not been 'saved'; or to the faithful as a result of persecution. Mental illness is seen as possession by an evil spirit or the devil (though it is easy today to explain that as simply a lack of medical knowledge). The suffering that is caused by the exploitation of the vulnerable by the rich and powerful is the result of human sin.

God is in control

I now listen to the BBC's Thought for the Day every day as I wait for the carers to arrive and get me up. Suffering is mentioned frequently (of course, it may simply be that I am more attuned to pick up on suffering as a subject). This is often in response to natural disasters – as with Mona Siddiqui quoted above – or in relation to famous individuals who have died or been diagnosed with serious illness. Catherine Pepinster concentrated on the tennis player Martina Navratilova, who had been diagnosed with breast cancer. Pepinster spoke of how, in winning fifty grand slam titles, Navratilova had needed total control of her life but that had now all changed:

> *The way she described her own reaction to the diagnosis was particularly striking: 'I feel so in control of my life and my body,' she said, 'then this comes and it is completely out of my hands.* [6]

Pepinster then brought in God:

> *It's often a crisis that causes us too to recognise that we rely on God and on one another. Being a great athlete like Martina Navratilova takes courage. But so too does having the humility to accept one's frailties and say 'I am no longer in control'.*

---

[6] Catherine Pepinster, Thought for the Day, 10 April 2010

Doesn't faith help?

At a personal level it might be comforting to hear at a young child's funeral that God had called that person early, but is that really so? (The most difficult funeral I ever took was where the parents thought they had been punished for their own sin.) If death was the result of an accident or illness with obvious cause and no human 'sin', why did it happen?

At the global disaster level, even if some natural phenomena may be broadly advantageous to our planet, why do hundreds or thousands die in an earthquake? Why do millions of people die of malaria each year? Yes, most cases could be prevented if the rich were less greedy and the enormous sums changing hands in the arms trade were used instead to fight malaria. But why did the mosquito evolve and why does disease exist? Where is our loving God?

Those are questions any scientist could dismiss fairly simply, whether or not they believed in God. Every part of creation is a segment in a chain, as the BBC Wildlife Magazine explains to non-experts like me. The diversity, uniqueness and inter-relatedness of the many parts of the natural world, from minute single-cell organisms to the earth's moving plates, leaves me in no doubt about how each is needed, or at least has a reason to exist in the process of evolution. That does not mean I see every single thing as God's direct creation, or I would be a vegetarian Buddhist examining each lettuce leaf for the possibility of a minute insect that I must avoid eating. If I were still able to eat, I might do that but for other reasons! Evolution is a fact, and fundamentalists who deny it have a problem in explaining how not everything in creation is good for us and can only surmise that God is testing us. The mosquito is a crucial foodstuff to birds we adore, even if it does harm to us; however, attributing the existence of a creature which benefits one part of creation but is bad for us to the action of the devil is very odd indeed.

So where am I?

So where am I on disease that strikes haphazardly? Good and bad both suffer, so it cannot be seen as punishment. It may be that a test brings out the best in both sufferer and carer – certainly the latter in my case – but I see no evidence in scripture for that. It is certainly not, in my case, anything to do with persecution – the New Testament prediction of persecution may be true in some parts of the world, but not in mine. Neither is it the result of exploitation by the rich – though I am certainly not a millionaire, I am one of the world's wealthy, but I am not punished for that.

Had more financial resources gone into medical research rather than funding military might around the world, perhaps stem-cell research would have started earlier and a cure would already have been found for Motor Neurone Disease. I can perhaps blame that delay on greed and lack of love between communities, but it still has no faith connection. Stem-cell research may be opposed by some faith communities but it is not divine intention or intervention that causes disease. Some suffering is accidental (whether from human or natural causes). Some is caused by other people – through violence, incompetence or greed – at international and personal levels. Some is self-inflicted, through drugs, alcohol, bad driving. Suffering can have benefits: greater sympathy for others, understanding of relationships, being better able to deal with other trauma. Perhaps the truth of that depends on the level of suffering or on the character of the individual.

Is God responsible? None of the hardship which I experience has to do with my faith or lack of it. Plenty of people, of all faiths or none, endure hardship – mental, physical or economic – and while some is self-inflicted for religious reasons, God is not responsible.

If we experience persecution, is it a sign that we have got it right? Is God testing us? Thinking of poor communities across the world, I have to answer 'No' to each of those questions. Faith does not protect them, either from other faiths or, in some cases, from governments. We hear interviews with the victims of earthquakes who have lost everything extolling how God will help them. That may be a sign of faith, but I am not sure it is what Jesus was trying to teach us. Are we being tested? And in which way? Again, it is the poorest who seem to be tested the most. Perhaps only they have the opportunity to go to heaven, and the rest of us are so rich, so self-centred, so uncaring that we have given up the right to join them.

So where are people like me? I certainly am not sinless – either now or (particularly) in my two marriage breakups but I do not believe I am being punished by God, nor being tested. My condition is not the result of sin. If I believed any of those to be the case I could not square that with a God who is supposed to be just. According to his own Son, the rich were the ones least likely to join him in heaven, so why do the exploiters of the poor not suffer? Most of us who, for example, buy cheap clothes from department stores have a part in this. Where is God in all that? Apart from giving people a hope of heaven and being part of a supportive community, there is little evidence that being a Christian helps to prevent physical suffering. Prayer may help psychologically, but through my whole life I have never heard anyone claim convincingly that God answered a specific request. Even meditation or a period of quiet contemplating a particular issue of suffering, with possibly a bible text in mind, may lead us to feel that God has intervened if a conclusion is reached; but while coming to a fresh understanding may make it easier to deal with personal suffering, God is changing nothing.

God is not punishing me, nor testing me: my condition is not the result of sin, and I am certainly not being persecuted. I am simply unlucky.

LIFE'S PURPOSE

I found nothing in scripture which provides me with a satisfactory answer to why we suffer. Even allowing for the Bible's dated understanding of the nature and causes of suffering, nothing helped. I am left only with some kind of scientific explanation.

I need another angle; and the first look has to be at the life of Jesus. Christians are right to feel that the suffering experienced by Jesus is horrendous, but this is a 'theological' horror, as Christians believe that God undergoes suffering for the whole of humanity. The torture and crucifixion of Jesus were at a level not unexpected in those days for a person seen to be a threat to the sensitive relationship between the local leadership and Rome. Jesus' suffering is vital to Christians – not because of its nature or severity, but because it was God acting for the whole human race. Persecution is part of the reaction of the powerful to challenges which threaten authority, culture and personal interests. Things have not changed!

Beyond needing to understand what God did on our behalf, is the Bible any use in dealing with living today? It is certainty the centre of many people's lives, and is used by many others as inspiration. It is part of nearly all church worship and the object of most Christian study. But it is also the cause of most disagreement and division between individuals and churches. An obvious example is homosexuality, which is dividing the Anglican Church. (I have a particular interest in this because of my previous work links with Latin America[1]) The same Church is also divided over the role of women in ministry, not helped by the Pope's interventions.

All this has made me explore exactly what I believe, to see whether the *life* of Jesus rather than his *death* has any importance for me. Should the followers of Jesus take their guidelines and priorities from his life rather than his death? Did his achievement of a sinless life lead to his Resurrection, and should correct believers emulate him? It may be obvious why this has emerged for me now, at least as a question, if not a hope. Have I changed position because I am dying? My personal beliefs have never really been questioned, even in the selection process for ordination. Assumptions were made by me, colleagues, authorities and those I was working for. People would question my interpretations of scripture but not my core faith – except when personal morality was rightly criticized. So, how did I get to where I am?

I need to go further back in my own life.

---

[1] I explain my views in 'Homophobia', available as a download from http://www.gileadbookspublishing.com/when-you-are-dying-additional-chapters.html

CHAPTER 5

Who Was I?

For everyone, understanding of one's early life is important because it helps explain aspects of later life. What emerges from the stories which follow is my enjoyment of being part of a group, coping with life's knocks and perhaps the origin of my leftish politics.

School was a very mixed experience. I passed the eleven plus, but I remember something my Primary School teacher told his class: 'it is better to be in the top stream of a Secondary Modern School than anything but the top stream of a Grammar School'. At the time we thought it was just an attempt to comfort those who failed the exam but, to some extent, he was right! I was told in my fourth year at Grammar School in Southampton that I would never make university so would have to be a teacher. The school appeared to be interested only in getting more Oxbridge and State Scholarships than the city's other boys-only Grammar School.

In the sixth form a teacher told us we now had an adult relationship and we could start by being honest about why we chose Economics as an A level subject. Foolishly, I believed him and said that another teacher had advised that it fitted the spaces in my timetable and my other subjects – History and Geography. My first essay was subsequently screwed up and thrown at me across the whole class and I was the only one who's Christian name he never used. I later wondered whether these were issues of class – I was the one person in my form who had to say weekly, 'Free school meals'. I was also the last in my year to move from shorts to long trousers.

The cub and scout troops I joined were not only classless but showed me how working in groups was important to me. The scouts were also responsible for my subsequent main hobby – bird watching. At that time scouts were allowed free camping anywhere in the New Forest; though most of my animal-watching was done alone or in small groups on day visits. My interest was then in deer, but having to keep quiet and still made me more aware of birds. At one time I hoped to work in forestry but again, school had a negative effect. I had been away sick when a science teacher told the class about chemical formula. After that I was pilloried by the teacher, was often the first to be asked to give a formula so he could get the class to laugh, and when a friend explained how it worked, I was accused of cheating. This set back my hopes and progress in science so much that it was impossible to do the relevant 'A' levels.

However, school was not an entirely negative experience. My history teacher, in particular, inspired all of us. I discovered that the church I attended was the first ever to be built by the Church of England (all others had previously been Roman Catholic). I wrote a history of the church and got the school's history prize.

The centre of life

Like many children of my generation, I was sent to Sunday school, which then had nearly as many pupils as would have gone to the Primary School where meetings were held. My parents never went to church but, having scrubbed us (in front of our only fire in the winter), we were dispatched and they had their only peaceful time together. The Sunday school children only went to church four times a year, and I think it was a Mothering Sunday when I noticed someone I knew in the choir. I joined. It opened a whole new world for me in music, liturgy, friends – and finance. I was not given any pocket money at home but close to the church was a large council estate built for families whose children were now of marriageable age. Often there were five or six weddings on a spring or summer Saturday. At half-a-crown a time I kept Woolworths going by buying jigsaws of railway engines and a toy shop was equally pleased to sell me bits for my model railway.

Wedding slots were allocated to choirboys as reward for good behaviour and attendance. The drawback was the longest section of the service with no singing – the sermon of the new vicar. Judging by the rapidly declining congregation, we were not the only ones bored stiff. We used to count the sections of sermon, all of which began 'And so ...' and if we didn't hear it we would leap to our feet and, in winter, hope that singing would warm us up.

As I moved into teenage years I found myself doing more and more in church, from serving at Eucharists to going in late on Saturday night to light the 24-hour candles over the altar so that they would be alight through all the Sunday services. I also melted down the remains of all the other candles to send back to suppliers. There were other more social reasons for keeping involved in the church. Most of my early playmates and all my early girlfriends came from church clubs. Those girlfriends ended my scout group connections.

Church was therefore at the centre of my life but, despite all the dull long sermons I had to endure, my interest in the religious rather than social side survived thanks to singing and what became a short-term obsession with high church liturgy. Thanks to my then girlfriend's sister, we found a beautiful

Norman church on the other side of Southampton. I remember in particular a Holy Week with lots of congregational involvement – bowing, genuflecting, singing and responding, crossing, kneeling, processing – which made me feel part of what was going on. I felt so involved that I don't even remember sermons at that church – though I do remember the priest's deeply resonant voice.

Ordination

No doubt partly because of this experience, I began to think I could do better – at least better than my home parish priest. But it was my deep-seated anger at a 'black mass' performed by an ex-school friend on the altar of a bombed church that made me certain I should be a priest.

I then had to go through the process of approval by the Winchester diocese. In a group of six or seven sixth-formers I was the only one not at public school. The only question I remember at the interview was about other interests; I mentioned John Donne and somebody made a joke about whether I preferred his romantic or later Christian poetry (I actually used to quote Donne in letters to my girlfriend and did not tell them I had never read the religious poems). I do not remember any theological questions – which was a good job, since I did not even have an O level GCE in Religious Education. There then followed a national residential selection weekend at which we were all convinced the most important thing was not to eat peas with a knife.

Despite my school's opinion, I got three good A levels, but without an O level in a foreign language they could not recommend a particular college. I did my own investigations and was accepted at Kings College in London, which I did not realize was then very liberal. I was quite excited to hear that Moses probably had not existed but, since someone must have been the Israelites' leader at different times, we might as well give all the leaders the same name and it might as well be Moses. Some students left after one term to go to more conservative colleges, but I remained fascinated! Lectures were largely enjoyable but there was a familiar disappointment there as well. Again, it was to do with sermons. The academics who preached seemed far more interested in impressing us with the titles of classic and contemporary writing they claimed to have read than in linking the Bible readings with anything particularly relevant to students or with what was going on in the real world.

I enjoyed what was totally new to me, but in the end I failed my finals, which I have always claimed was because of training to row at Henley Regatta in my final year. That may have been a contributing factor but loneliness was probably the main reason. 'Digs' were allocated by the college, usually at a vicarage, but when I realised that black people were not admitted into the house I stayed in – even wedding and Baptism interviews were conducted in the porch – I had to leave. That meant leaving a fellow student and finding a place by myself. It was a good place but far from colleagues; my studies suffered.

Family influence

To understand both the story so far and my later life, it will help to explore my family's influence. My father died more than 50 years ago, when I was thirteen. He was an erect former soldier – twelve years in India, rising to the rank of band corporal – who became a policeman in the UK. From when I was about six he was obviously ill, either in hospital for two major lung operations or recuperating from them (I remember seeing the huge scars). I recall we children only visited him once, in the hospital garden – perhaps children were then not allowed into the wards, or were our parents protecting us? My father did return to police work on light duties in Southampton Docks – I remember my elder brother starting Dad's motorbike every working morning as he was too weak to do it himself. Towards the end he looked a bit like a holocaust victim, made worse because he was nearly six foot three inches tall and always slim.

I have no memory of my mother talking to any of us three children about his illness, and certainly not about the possibility of death – and I don't recall any conversation with my brother or sister about such a possibility. Once through my parents' bedroom door I heard him say, perhaps deliberately loudly, 'They need to be told I'm dying'. Perhaps that was why I was eventually allowed into his bedroom once in his last few weeks. I was sent to choir practice the day he died and to school rather than to his funeral. It was as if this was a normal thing which I needed not to worry about and could deal with on my own. Auto-protection worked well: I didn't cry. I remember asking with my brother to watch television soon after our father's death and then seeing Mum folded over in an armchair, seeming half her size and looking as we'd never seen her before. She had coped with years of care for someone she had seen decline to a shadow of his former self and saved us from so much; we now seemed callous – wanting TV rather than joining her in grief.

I never knew of my father's suffering. Perhaps my mother found things so hard that she could not share her own feelings or was trying to protect us. I do not recall her ever talking about feelings or relationships. Above all, she felt life was so private that even within the family we should keep things to ourselves. A classic example was many years later when she fell and damaged a wrist. She walked up a one-in-six hill, then a mile or so to her GP, who sent her to Accident and Emergency, which she did by bus. The hospital admitted her but postponed treatment for several days because of high blood pressure, not helped by walking up that hill. At that time I was living with my wife and children just a few miles away and could have picked her up from home, but the first I heard from her was the following day when she rang from her hospital bed asking me to get some personal things from home. She didn't like fuss.

Maybe my lack of long-term friends, my loneliness at university and my later unwillingness to attempt to run a parish on my own are in part influenced by my mother. But on the positive side, maybe my patience in the slow writing of this book has the same source. I have 'progressed' through various kinds of computer technology after first managing slowly with my left hand. I then used a silvery dot on the bridge of my nose which was picked up by a camera on top of my laptop; this followed my head movement and meant I could move a cursor around an on-screen keyboard. My capacity to use this slowed down as my neck muscles froze, and for a while I couldn't 'type'. Now I have the system which picks up eye movement. Patience is certainly needed as each letter can take several seconds, sometimes much longer.

Patience is also needed in daily life as I can do nothing except breathe and move my eyes. I cannot contribute to any conversations – especially frustrating in the early days if I knew the answer to questions being raised. Food was another issue. I used to enjoy cooking, especially baking, and enjoyed eating the results. My pleasure now is in sitting at the table watching Gaby having a good time, sharing a meal with friends and conversing in a way now impossible with me. Ultimately, of course, this is the time waiting to die. So if patience is in my blood from my mother, thanks Mum!

These traits I inherited, or perhaps learned through my upbringing, also relate to important choices made in my adult life – which begins with my life-changing first experience of Africa.

Namibia – another influence

When I failed the necessary exams, the Church organisation responsible for theological training suggested I take a break and, among other possibilities, mentioned the next-door missionary society, USPG. Therefore in 1968, instead of pastoral training and ordination, I got married and went to Namibia (then 'South West Africa', occupied by South Africa and under the same apartheid system – segregated schools, very little higher education for black students, and English viewed as a dangerous language to allow young people to learn as it gave them access to alternative ideas).

My original job was in a white-only but supposedly liberal English-medium school run by the Anglican Church. Shortly after we arrived a new headmistress was appointed, who we later realized had left another African country because she would not accept black rule. She and I did not get on, and I was eventually sacked. The reason was that I had worked with some boarders to turn an area of bare rock at the school entrance into a wildlife garden. At the end of term they told their parents what they had done and were told in return, 'That is black people's work' and – which was worse – black people had seen them do it! So I had to go (this would not have been allowed had the bishop been around, but he was fundraising in the USA).

This turned out to have a positive outcome. Following a temporary job with a bookseller (which gave me an interesting view of South African censorship) as missionaries, we were eventually allowed into one of the Bantustans (areas that black people were compelled to live in). This was Ovamboland in the far north of the country. There I was appointed Principal of the only English-medium high school for black students in the whole country, run by the Anglican Church. It was disliked by the government, as understanding English gave the students access to alternative views such as those found on the BBC. We were not allowed to teach the third and final year, so we crammed everything inside two years and entered ourselves as a private exam centre. The church's role in the independence struggle has been well documented and undoubtedly the school changed the pupils' lives – many now have important roles in the state of Namibia – but it changed mine too.

Those three years in Namibia gave direction to my future life in many ways, as I experienced both another culture and an evil government. I was certainly aware of the suffering of the black majority and it made me want to see things change at home too. I remained involved in Namibian affairs back in the UK, and was banned by the South African government for twenty one years (that was political – probably the result of being interviewed on the BBC World Service). But my overriding motivation came from one man – Colin Winter. He was Dean of the cathedral in the capital, Windhoek, which is said to be the smallest in the world. The day we arrived, we learned that the bishop was being deported and Colin was to succeed him. The Anglican Church, unlike most other denominations, was not divided by race and the majority-black clergy voted to a man for Colin. Other candidates had ignored issues of race, inequality and poverty, and the church's responsibility to tackle them, instead stressing personal faith. For them this meant avoiding anything which involved the church in any conflict with government. The black majority of laity also saw this as hidden support for apartheid and joined the clergy in voting for Colin Winter.

Colin was a charismatic leader, but particularly a preacher who inspired me by relating belief to real life. That, along with his writing and activity, was why opponents and the government were glad to get rid of him five years later. And it was his sermons which persuaded me to continue to ordination and at least try to make my sermons relevant to the present, the community I was part of and the issues they faced.

Parish ministry

I went back to King's College, got a first class award in the uniquely Anglican AKC (Associate of King's College), had a year's not-exactly-brilliant pastoral training in Canterbury and, after ordination, went to a parish in Walthamstow in east London. There I learned an important fact: the local working class liked my imitation-Colin Winter sermons while the middle class, who tended to live outside the parish, disliked what I said.

I spent part of my time there as a college chaplain. It got me out of some parish duties, but I found it difficult because I was not very good at 'small talk', or starting conversations with strangers – the same reason I found parish work hard to do. I didn't know what to say to a student in a bar or when visiting a parishioner for no particular reason. The exception was one old lady who had a weekly home communion visit; she was full of fun stories and I managed to get her a free emergency phone. The rest I found difficult, especially speaking to any bereaved family before the funeral.

It was then usual to do three years in an initial 'curacy' but I escaped after two, when funding was found to work for a year for Colin Winter, who had by then been deported. This was much more my 'cup of tea', working with Namibian students and travelling round the country, talking and preaching about racism and Namibia.

I then had four years in Leicester. Within a team of five (including retired, part-time and non-stipendiary clergy) I was technically the 'senior curate', and it was assumed I would want to be in charge of a corrugated-iron roofed 'daughter church', originally built for local workers and the servants of those attending the more magnificent parish church. Most curates would have seen this as good supervised training for future parish responsibilities, but I did not want to be in that position. I didn't see it as the way a team should work – but beneath this, undoubtedly, was the frightening prospect of a future working on my own. So I managed to persuade the vicar that I should instead work in both churches, concentrating on youth work, which was good in Leicester. On Sunday evening large numbers attended church, where I designed a series of five separate groups which they could move through according to age and maturity. It started at 5.30 pm with the youngest and ended when the pub closed. As in many churches, the 'family service' was a compromise between what the adults wanted and what the children wanted, and was largely boycotted by both. I began a monthly special service in the church hall, which proved so popular that even adults who had no children began to attend. We also had night walks and week-long treks.

I spoke at schools and became the Bishop's unofficial adviser on sects which were then persuading vulnerable young people to give up all they possessed and preventing families from being in touch. I also spent a while teaching for both secondary exam levels in Religious Education at a local girls' school. As always, I worked well with groups but had few close relationships.

My theological training had included learning how to help a family deal with a relative's body if they preferred a priest to do this – such things as closing eyes with old penny coins and blocking various orifices to stop bits of leakage. No-one ever asked me to do any of those things. However, in Leicester I did a huge number of funerals – though without pastoral involvement. Due to lack of cooperation from funeral directors, unless relatives requested it, parishes of the deceased were not identified and clergy were instead on a rota at the crematorium and did not know the families or even the cause of death. Most of the deceased would be people with no church connection whose relatives wanted a ritual for a formal end, with perhaps the hope that they might meet again one day. I would have a standard short sermon, explaining why I wore white rather than the conventional black stole. This would follow the reading from Revelation 21: 1-7 (a vision of heaven) and I would speak very briefly about hope for the future. Whether they or I truly believed this, it was the right and expected thing to say, then. On the way out, as they queued to look at wreaths I would shake people's hands and mumble appropriate sympathy but keep an eye on the time, as each funeral was allotted only twenty minutes in total and I would probably have the next one on my rota. I would certainly have been more anxious if there had been any pastoral involvement – even though only a few families would be from my parish.

After four years in Leicester I went back to the city of my youth – Southampton – as Team Vicar for Religious Education. The team had seven members, three of whom had pastoral responsibilities in the parish, and the rest of us had responsibility for the whole city in areas such as industrial chaplaincy and R.E.. It had formerly been six parishes, but a mixture of war-time bombing and immigration by people of other faiths meant that only two churches were in regular use; one of the surplus churches was used by the Greek Orthodox and another caused controversy as the first Anglican church building in England to be sold to another faith. And - guess what! One of the two churches still in use was that Norman church which had kept me going all those years before. I spent most of my time running a Resource Centre and having fun helping out in schools, particularly trying to give confidence where there was no RE specialist. I really enjoyed working with kids without having overall responsibility for discipline, and got to know some schools very well – one year I remember being invited to fourteen different Nativity Plays. I was not expected to promote any particular view and would say, 'Some Christians believe this....' or 'We hold resources on a number of faiths and views within them'.

After this the usual career move would have been to take charge of a parish but I never wanted to be in such a post (leaving this particular job was the result of a marriage breakup which was stupid and entirely my fault; that obviously affected timing). The reason I always gave for my choice was that I preferred working in teams – and that is partly true. I had kept going by working in situations which did not concentrate on pastoral matters to do with the beginning and end of life. I found it difficult to relate, but I am sure that was only part of the reason why, in my ten years in parishes, I had avoided most of the normal duties.

The relationships which seemed to work were with people at a distance – teachers in particular. I was generally good with groups and not devoid of ideas, but not good one-to-one. It was not that I had bad relationships, but l usually required a reason to speak. My future jobs allowed me to develop that further – especially in interviewing.

A major change

After those ten years in parishes I moved on to USPG, a mission agency; not because I wanted to swell the numbers of believers but because of my concern for justice in southern Africa. It was as a Regional Desk Officer that I visited forty-seven countries, mainly in Latin America, the Caribbean and Africa; met many extraordinary people, and saw much poverty. I spent a total of twenty years working mainly to recruit and support or advise people about working abroad in mission or development, all but three of those years with religious charities[1]. These jobs enabled me to concentrate on action rather than doctrine. Also I could again avoid the parochial issues – not that they were missing in overseas churches, but it was not my job to sort them out, and instead I was required to concentrate on training, funding, and finding staff or volunteers.

---

[1] I wrote Working in Development, published in 2007 by World Service Enquiry (part of Christians Abroad, of which I was Director for seven years). ISBN 978-0-9558393-0-6

Defining my beliefs

So were all these job choices just circumstantial? As Christians, all our views are influenced by our interpretation of scripture as well as by personal experience and the views of those who have been important in our lives. Reflecting on the previous chapters on suffering and then the history of my working life has led me to think more deeply about what is important to me. My mind is not occupied by thoughts of an afterlife – rather, I have been trying to understand the faith world, to put myself together. I do not think that problems are solved by prayer but by considered action, so I want to use the time remaining to me to consider that action and to sort out for the first time what I believe. It may seem odd that someone who has been involved in the Church since the age of eight needs to define his beliefs though perhaps, if some other Christians were pressed, I might not be found to be so unusual.

I am dying. I am paralysed from the neck down and have sessions of coughing, choking and weak breathing. I am completely dependent on others for survival. Gaby gives me loving care; it is this which makes life worth hanging on to. But what is going to happen to us when we die? Should that be the priority life-issue for Christians? The way to discover what has been important to me – including my choice of jobs – is to investigate what I have said in sermons. I never kept a diary or wrote a longer account of feelings or thoughts, so sermons are the one clue to what I was feeling or what was important.

Colin Winter again

My theological development over the years has been influenced by many experiences, and especially by visiting overseas Churches where suffering and early death are almost expected; but what I have preached over those years has, I hope, been based, however badly, on that man who changed my life – Colin Winter.

I began to preach in Namibia, then in those three parishes, followed by all those USPG years, including speaking in USPG-supporting parishes in the UK and frequent invitations to preach in many overseas churches. At home I worshipped with Gaby for over ten years in a predominantly West African congregation in south east London, and preached regularly there. A variety of places, congregations, situations and challenges. So, claiming I prioritized the active side of Christian life, what did I actually say and what do I want to say now from my experience?

When I first thought of writing a book it was going to be my 'ten last sermons' – ten things which were important to me. While some of these subjects do appear in the following chapters, it has turned out a bit differently – very personal and not necessarily objective. Sermons have been important in my life, and looking at some I preached in former years was surprisingly liberating; it made me not only connect with the story of my life but, for the first time, acknowledge what I truly believe. That is especially relevant now as I think of life, death and the future – all of which leads to 'Selfish Salvation'.

CHAPTER 6

Selfish Salvation

Discovery

Looking back over thirty-seven years of sermons, I have to confess that I discovered that I seem to have avoided preaching about doctrine at major moments in the church's year – whether Christmas, Good Friday, Easter, Ascension or Pentecost. While these celebrations are vital in holding together the communities of local and global church fellowships, I have always preached somewhat sideways sermons. I thought this might be because I imagined people had heard it all before or because I wanted to replace expositions with either a celebration of joy or, in the case of Good Friday, feelings of sorrow and guilt.

But reading and then thinking through those sermons, it is clear that the reason for my slant has been, instead, my own discomfort. That discomfort has been around what conventional Christianity says about these core events of our Christian year – what we have to believe in order to be called 'Christian'. Individually the sermons were usually well accepted, but collectively they show that I had another priority, a different agenda.

My Christmas sermons have often been about parts of the story relating to the incarnation but not about the birth of the Son of God. Mary has come into it a lot, but never as the holy, perfect, obedient model so often portrayed to us. She would be that teenage girl, probably suffering all the exclusion that any single mother would feel in many cultures. The flight to Egypt, linked to any current arguments on asylum-seeking, would come into it sometimes. There would always be comparisons with whatever community I was then part of. The story would be linked to Christian behaviour and priorities, and not with the facts of the birth of a son of divine origin.

Good Friday was always about how obvious it was that humans would react in such a way. Just as in today's celebrity culture people who do things the public want are hailed as heroes, in the ministry of Jesus it would be miracles and healing as well as his pronouncements by which people were inspired. But, just as the press and people turn against celebrities today who no longer fit in, so it was with Jesus. He had gone too far in his ethical and moral demands, and it was easy for the spiritual and political leaders to whip up crowd support. Less than a week before, according to the Christian calendar, Jesus had been welcomed enthusiastically on what we now call Palm Sunday. Celebrities may only be figuratively killed off, but for Jesus it was an obvious and predictable result. He asked too much, and Barabbas was far less demanding. My sermon would focus on what our faith asks of us today, and which of those two 'celebrities' we would have shouted for in front of Pontius Pilate.

Easter was much more difficult. Other faiths have God's infallible 'word', as many Christians believe the Bible to be. They have prophecy and moral certainty, but none of the other faiths has God taking human form, living for thirty-plus years, dying, and coming to life again on this earth. Without specific reference to belief, my sermons would be about how Jesus made a difference to those who felt his presence. Disciples who had known him felt a reassuring presence and therefore wished to follow his example – a model for us today. Perhaps Luke 24:21 would raise some questions about what we want for our society today - 'We had been hoping that he was the man to liberate Israel' (NEB). Considering Resurrection reports, the disciples clearly reflected on the Jesus they knew when alive, whom they had hoped would change their own lives; there is no suggestion of them believing they or later Christians would also rise from the dead.

Ascension was easier; again, not about facts or doctrine, but about the need for Christianity to become more than a collection of followers of a present celebrity. In one sense this was the most important festival for me – Jesus is not physically with us. This was therefore the bringing together of all that was important to me – Christian behaviour, what faith asks of us today, and how Jesus is the model. Without the physical presence of the leader of any faith, the followers have responsibility to be leaders themselves. It would be a key element in many mission-based sermons, linked often to the training people had done before going overseas with USPG which then had its training base at the 'College of the Ascension'.

Pentecost would be easier too, as the confirmation of our responsibility; containing both the promise of an international church and the seeds of the present divisions within it, as groups and individuals claim that the Holy Spirit is guiding them and their actions. (I know a bishop in Latin America - sadly a British missionary - who insists that none of his clergy can correctly hold opinions which differ from anything on which he pronounces, as his selection and consecration were 'the work of the Spirit'. Discussions are pointless and cannot themselves be 'inspired'.) In contrast I would speak of how St. Peter's sermon at Pentecost (Acts 2:14-36) interprets the events of that day as being for everyone – slaves and free, young and old. All are found among the long list of peoples present, of which only one group comes from Europe, the rest from Africa and Asia – a point not lost on those who say that this story, like much else, has since been hijacked by the North. So which model then? And which now best exemplifies the church which we should be part of? Do we all need the same model? What can we learn from each other?

Most of these points were made to congregations linked with USPG – at the time I had done some sabbatical research on what we northerners can learn from the church in the south. But when I was working in the parishes, I would concentrate on our having been given a conscious mind and the necessity of taking time to listen to what is happening inside our heads.

Act correctly

Looking back, I nearly always spoke of the need for Christians to act correctly. I avoided explaining the doctrines of major festivals, feeling that it was more important to stress what they meant in the light of whatever was in the news that week. I also found that I followed Jesus – at least in method – by seeking the underlying principle rather than detailed and irrelevant rules (the subject of the following chapter).

I am not trying to say that there are no Christians who believe in political and social action who also believe in traditional doctrines such as the Resurrection and in the power of prayer. There are many such heroic people that I come nowhere near in terms of commitment. For instance, in the missionary diocese of Namibia (then called Damaraland) three bishops in succession were deported by the South African government, local leaders were tortured, and the seminary where I taught was destroyed by the South African army. I am sure those people wanted and worked towards change. I am also sure they saw the Resurrection as giving them a hope of heaven, but this was a hope and not a motive.

In adjoining South Africa, Desmond Tutu has to be the finest example of a person with belief in the traditional doctrines – he said that if thousands of people were praying for the end of the injustice of apartheid then no secular body could win out against that. I admire him as the greatest example of how we all should be – in recent years he has been speaking out on everything from his government's strange position on Zimbabwe to the Anglican Church's divisions on homosexuality and the role of women.

In Latin America the government-assassinated Archbishop Romero is another outstanding example of a leader whose faith and action were inextricably linked.

None would say that any of those people – bishops or lay people – acted in order to obtain salvation, but because their faith gave them high values which they needed to apply to their own situation. I admire them; they all have something remarkable – faith and action – but surely there are people of other faiths or none who demonstrate the same depth of belief and are equally active?

The basis of faith

Any web search on 'statements of faith' will lead to hundreds of links, mostly to small evangelical churches, but major denominations appear as well. A Roman Catholic site suggests we look at the Nicene Creed, with its traditional outlining of Incarnation, Death, Resurrection and Ascension. This is also used in daily worship in much of the Anglican Church. The Baptist Union web site suggests the following as its 'Basis' at the beginning of its 'Declaration of Principle':

1. That our Lord and Saviour Jesus Christ, God manifest in the flesh, is the sole and absolute authority in all matters pertaining to faith and practice, as revealed in the Holy Scriptures, and that each Church has liberty, under the guidance of the Holy Spirit, to interpret and administer His laws.

2. That Christian Baptism is the immersion in water into the Name of the Father, the Son, and the Holy Ghost, of those who have professed repentance towards God and faith in our Lord Jesus Christ who 'died for our sins according to the Scriptures; was buried, and rose again the third day'.

The piece about 'liberty to interpret' is interesting and different from the Roman Catholic hierarchical approach but, Baptism and Eucharistic theologies apart, the same basic doctrines are there as in most major churches.

I certainly agree that the words of Jesus have authority – though, as I will argue in Chapter 7, 'Principles or Rules', this has to be seen in cultural context. But I now realise that for me, believing in the whole Creed does not matter. I do not see Jesus as my salvation-bringer, as 'Messiah' in the traditional way. The way I see the messiahship is different, and to underline that I will use the term 'following Jesus'. I believe that if the world practised Jesus' teaching we would change things for ever and his followers should see that call as paramount. If our actions were to bring us salvation, then that would be wonderful – but that cannot be a motivation. That would be against the commands of Jesus; it would be selfish.

The trend in many churches appears to be in the opposite direction, making active faith subsidiary to what you must believe in order to gain personal salvation. Faith is concentrated on believing in those Christian calendar events, and in what happened to Jesus. The result for us will be something called heaven. That belief is more important than following the wider ethical demands of Jesus the man, who told us very clearly what we should do and how we should behave.

Resurrection

The Resurrection is at the core of Christianity and is also the hardest challenge for anyone advocating the literal truth of the Bible or the authority of the traditional Christian Creeds. The Gospel accounts are so different – both in historical terms of the event itself and the later 'appearances', and also in the portrayal of Jesus – that there are certainly questions for me about their legitimacy in recording a real 'happening'.

Mary Magdalene features in Mark and John, the first and last Gospels to be written. In Mark she is accompanied by two other women, carrying spices to anoint the body. In John she is alone, talks to a 'gardener' whom she suddenly recognises as the risen Christ, then reports to Peter. He, with the 'beloved disciple', runs to see the empty tomb but says and does nothing. The same strange silence is kept by the women in Mark, who run away scared, and are not recorded as having passed on the message about going on to Galilee given by the figure they meet in the tomb. In Luke the discovery by the (different?) women is reported but not believed by the disciples. In Matthew alone there are guards who report that Jesus' body has been stolen.

As the last Gospel to be written, John not only deals with the life and actions of Jesus in a more theological and less historical way (doctrine by then being more important than the events, which were already recorded and believed in) but also has many unique stories. These include the resurrection of Lazarus and the story of Thomas. Despite his wanting to touch Jesus, there is no clear proof this happened, or that Jesus is really present. In most of the appearances in the three other Gospels it is equally not clear that the presence of Jesus is seen to be that of a real person. Mark's tale is the most dramatic, with the women fleeing in terror once they have witnessed the empty tomb. Luke has the most appearances, including the account of the Emmaus journey, which gives the writer the chance to show how all that had happened fitted in with Old Testament prophecy, with the unrecognised Jesus telling the story. He also has the account of Jesus eating to show that this is a real human being. Elsewhere this figure seems ghost-like and frightening and able to appear and vanish through walls, and is often unrecognised. Yet the Lazarus story of his being returned to life by Jesus includes evidence of renewed normal life and recognition.

The Resurrection stories suggest that the memory of Jesus lived on in some way and that he had made an incredible impact on his early followers. But what actually happened had already become a matter of faith and oral history. The mostly illiterate people then had much better story memories than most of us today, and they would not have been unaware of the differences between the accounts. What was important for me as a preacher were the implications of their belief – a 'myth' in so many ways. Many Christian leaders now tell us we should believe in the 'fact' of resurrection rather than in the implications of what the person Jesus would want of us.

Behind all this is undoubtedly something people will rightly call my lack of faith. From their viewpoint, I have to admit that is true. Despite my physical condition, and certainly not changed by it, I do not know what will happen to me after death. It would be wonderful to believe in my own resurrection, to have faith that it will not all end here, and that there will be continuing relationships. But I am not sure. I am not prepared to dismiss those who believe, but my own faith-based activities and thoughts are not dependant on belief in an after-life as a prize for following Jesus.

Priorities

Of course, I don't properly follow Jesus either. I believe I should, and that he is the greatest spiritual, community and ethical leader the world has seen. I should do more. But I am much more disturbed by the way a religious wrap-around was quickly applied by those who worked on and diluted his Principles in developing doctrine and church rules, and the way this has continued as churches divide and detail their own beliefs. Some dilution can be explained by the culture and understanding of the time but so much has been extrapolated which is counter to the whole basis of Jesus' teaching and therefore to the life which he wanted us to live. Instead of helping me and others with how we deal with modern life, churches spend their time on internal divisions – at least, that is how it comes across.

A domestic example is in the change from the British Council of Churches (BCC) to the Churches Together in Britain and Ireland (CTBI). The BCC addressed national and international issues with statements, meetings and consultations. It was usually quite radical. The CTBI was developed from the BCC to bring in more members but in doing so, it lost the right to speak out unless all members agreed. The time this process takes has silenced what used to bring an interesting angle to many issues. I used to be involved in several regional 'Forums' dealing with overseas regions, in which the relevant Christian agencies could meet regularly, discuss and issue statements. That right was removed, and with staff support taken away, the Forums slowly ceased to attract members and were eventually closed down. Priorities had changed. By concentrating on devolving to four national bodies and helping churches learn more about each other (not in themselves wrong aims) it has become gutless.

In many ways, churches and Christian groups seem preoccupied with issues that have little support in the outside world. In 2008 the Anglican Church's disagreements were centre-stage, in the Christian media in particular, but other news stories included questions about the power of the Roman Catholic Church, which is seen by some to be destroying lives. In Nicaragua, for example, where no abortion is allowed, women die in pregnancy and are forced to have the children of their rapists. As described in the prelude to the next section, in many parts of Africa the effect of disallowing the use of condoms to help to control the spread of AIDS is a significant cause of death. In the USA, Christianity and right-wing politics are linked on those same issues. Meanwhile, the belief in the need to have a 'Holy Land' in order that the second coming of Jesus should happen is the basis of support for the occupation of Palestine, and for military action in the region. I once met members of an American sect in Central America which believed that destroying the environment would help to bring the second coming - something they wanted soon.

Neither is my struggle, hope and wish that I could believe in a conventional way helped by opinions within the Church such as those quoted above, or by stress on minutiae of biblical interpretation, both of which ignore the main thrust of the teacher they purport to follow. So many individuals and groups claim they alone have the real faith, and therefore the real path to salvation, and insist that there is no true knowledge of God outside Christianity. Saddest of all are those who tell their followers that only believing in their version of things will bring them salvation. We witness little of the love of neighbour, the demonstration that often it is those outside faith who have the clearest understanding of how we should behave towards others. Belief IN Jesus seems to be enough – as long as a particular line is followed.

Faith can be selfish

What concerns me most is not just that doctrinal differences and ethical demands have become so divisive, but more that the basis of such faith is selfish. A faith which proclaims that only its own members, 'we', can be saved, is hard enough to swallow; the idea that anyone who emphasizes that 'I' will be saved by what 'I' believe and centres their life on that aim is surely selfish – and to me indigestible. It seems as though, were I to change and claim to believe in all those things I will not preach about, then I would be 'saved'. Motivation, behaviour, views on world problems – all are irrelevant. This is despite the words recorded in Matthew 7:21 that not everyone who calls Jesus 'Lord, Lord' will enter the Kingdom of Heaven, but only those who do what the Father in heaven wants them to do. The parable a few verses later of houses built on sand and rock clearly indicates that following the words of Jesus is the same as doing what the Father requires. Following those commands, doing what God/Jesus requires, is the hard rock. That is the real foundation for individuals and for the world.

Any search for Gospel references to 'faith' or 'belief' will show links to individual healing. Mark 9: 24-29 is classic in this respect. Disciples fail to heal a child with an evil spirit; Jesus says everything is possible for the person who has faith, but does not mention himself. The father of the child is honest and, in many senses, is to me a good example for us all. 'I do have faith, but not enough. Help me to have more!' The child is healed. Then Jesus heals two blind men who also say that they believe he can heal them, but do not express more than that.

The case of the officer's servant (Matthew 8:5-13) may seem a little different. The officer does not require Jesus to come to his house and instead explains his own parallel understanding of authority ('I order this one, 'Go' and he goes'). His faith is in Jesus as the authority as well as the transmitter of healing. Jesus recognises here a faith he has not found anywhere in Israel.

In these and so many other examples, faith seems to be around the reputation and ability of the person of Jesus, but does not require faith in him as the Son of God or the only saviour. To take this further, to have a healing of our planet, our concentration should not be on following Jesus in order to 'go to heaven' but, in the power of his words, we should improve the lives of those around us. Our capacities are now greater than ever before and to change our world would be a greater 'miracle' than any of Jesus' individual healings.

Paul takes the idea further. Faith is about learning what to do. In fact, *'God puts people right through their faith in Jesus Christ. God does this to all who believe in Christ, because there is no difference at all: everyone has sinned and is far away from God's saving presence'* (Romans 3:22-23, GNB). Faith, in this context, has to include action or it is not real.

A counter-argument

Any honest text-searching is likely to find something to go against whatever one is advocating. Romans 10:6-17 is as clear an example as any. Commenting on Moses' command (Leviticus: 18:5) to obey the law in order to live, Paul can be interpreted as suggesting something different. It is not about keeping the commands of Jesus (the new law), but about confession of faith. *'If you confess that Jesus is Lord and believe that God raised him from death, you will be saved'* (Romans 10:9, GNB).

How do I deal with that – something which seems to say that the important thing is to have faith in Jesus in order to be saved? Ignoring it would be one way; something done by so many of us when we want to sidestep other demands in the New Testament. Or I can find a way round it in the same or similar texts. Here it would be possible to do this by saying that the wider theme is really to justify Paul's mission to the Gentiles. All are equal if they have the same faith (which is the theme of the following section, beginning from 10:13, 'Everyone who calls out to the Lord for help will be saved', and continuing through the whole of the following chapter and beyond). But whatever the wider theme, the words are still there.

Another way round is a little more helpful to my argument. 'God's message is near you, on your lips and in your heart - that is the message of faith that we preach' (10:8). I could argue that the message in the heart has to include concern for others in the way that Jesus would have commanded, referring to Mt. 7:21.

The truth is that we accept those parts of scripture which attract us, support our argument or help us personally, and we struggle with those which go against what we hope for. St. Paul undoubtedly believed what he wrote. So I will be honest and admit that the priority for me is that the message of Jesus is about the way we should relate to each other in this world, and about his broad ethical Principles; not the detailed things he said which may relate only to his own culture and time. And just as there are some awful bits of the Old Testament that we choose to ignore (which present God as a kind of ethnic cleanser and destroyer of the innocent) so I can ignore those specific words of Romans 10 because our faith should have matured in the years since Paul wrote. We have learned more, we live in a different world, and those who argue for the continuing influence of the Holy Spirit should surely see that we might have been given guidance since New Testament times. Is not the Holy Spirit the equal presence of God?

I do not see my fate beyond death as being any different because I do not accept particular passages of scripture – they are all an attempt to understand what was then going on, and we are still doing that today. In our continuing struggle to learn what it is right to do, the biblical books and especially the commands of Jesus are highly important, but we have to relate them to our current situation.

To see Romans 10 as the core of Christianity – to say that the purpose of our earthly lives is to gain eternal life (as an aim rather than an outcome), and that for this to happen we have to believe in something very specific – seems to me immoral. It is made worse by those many churches which see only their own interpretation of particular doctrines as the way to eternal life. Those who do not follow their straight line, however much they might say 'I confess that Jesus is Lord' will not get there; 'Join us, and you will.'

I have heard so many sermons on receiving what we ask for -

often assumed to be material things. *'Ask and you will receive'* (Matthew 7:7, NEB) is seen to be a matter of faith – believe it and, like salvation, it will come. That is just one example of the selfish, selective faith we are often encouraged to follow. It ignores the second of the sayings in the same series, *'Seek and you will find'*. Asking alone ignores its context, which changes things entirely. Once we have sought the truth, and found the way that Jesus wanted us to be, then no asking could ever be for ourselves. So I am not praying for personal recovery. My faith in the NHS, local social services and the hospice to help me through to my end is greater than my belief in prayer or in any reward to believers simply because of what they believe.

Morality or myth?

For traditionalists, faith without proof is the important bit. Faith in an Incarnation and Resurrection that cannot be proven are the hallmark for them. While we can choose to trust some intuition on this, we can 'prove' nothing. So for someone who is not prepared to see either biblical texts or later theologies in themselves as proof, there has to be something else. Faith was important for the early Christian community, for whom the life of Jesus had to fit both Old Testament predictions and contemporary views of life and after-life. If we do not accept their worldview, then we have to discover whether there is something else that fits our present lives. The best way of doing this is to analyse what should affect us today – not dated views of the universe and the divine place within it, but something which makes a difference to our lives today. Morality is far more important than myth. It is about changing the lives we live and so changing our world today, rather than explaining the world. Myths of Creation,

Incarnation and Resurrection may be important, but belief in them has no point if it makes no difference to our lives.

Matthew 25, the parable of the sheep and the goats, helps on this. While of its time, and demonstrating belief in Resurrection, the future has nothing to do with faith. Those who thought that believing the right thing was all that was required were deeply shocked. The story is wonderful to contemplate – no-one got what they expected, neither sheep nor goat. But those who knew how to behave, to follow God's commands perhaps even without knowing him, were rewarded for being closer to him than those who claimed they believed the 'right' thing.

I cannot accept doctrines that have nothing to do with the life that Jesus intended for us to live. Personal faith based on a belief that it will bring eternal life, with or without certain behaviour, is a selfish attitude to salvation. I want to follow the person Jesus because I believe he had things to say which collectively mean more for our planet, our human lives, relationships and future than any other leader. He may be the Son of God, he may have risen from the dead, he may have ascended into heaven, and there might be eternal life. If heaven exists, then if we follow the commands of Jesus we might get there. That salvation would be wonderful, but it cannot be the reason for being a follower.

Obviously not all who believe in the way I have caricatured do so because they are selfish, but increasingly we are being divided and given choices around very specific dogmas, rules and practices. We learn that personal salvation comes from following a strict code of belief and dictates rather than through personal commitment. The question for me is how much such beliefs have anything to do with the Principles that Jesus expounded. In the next chapter I will try to explain in more detail why I believe these Principles are vital and how the development of doctrine has taken away our churches' focus. I will then explore how Jesus both spoke on and demonstrated what these Principles were.

So I am not concerned that in my preaching I avoided saying we must believe that Jesus is the Son of God, or that his Resurrection has guaranteed that those who believe will follow him to heaven. That notion goes against his own preaching. It is selfish salvation.

CHAPTER 7

Principles or Rules

Well, that's over. The first time I have really expressed things that have been around for a long time. Or maybe the first time I have thought through the reasons behind the way I preached or even the way I have worked. Looking back, it is still surprising that I got to where I did. I have no memory of a 'vocation'. I did think I could do better than my childhood vicar, and that may have started me off – but it was Colin Winter who got me going again.

Text or Context?

The thinking for this chapter began with recalling a sermon I gave to a largely West African congregation in south-east London. Many had a good knowledge of the Bible – indeed, on any bus going to work in the morning there would always be five or six people, usually women and usually black, reading their Bibles. Sometimes there were notes or guides, but usually it was just the text. Many in the congregation would know huge chunks of text but would not always know its context.

The gospel reading for the day was Luke 9:1-6. When I discovered that, I must admit my first thought was: 'Oh, no, not that again!' For the twelve years I worked for USPG, a major part of the job was to recruit, send and support missionaries for southern Africa, Latin America and the Caribbean. As part of the job I was often asked to preach, and that gospel reading was a favourite choice for their commissioning or their final home-church event before they went off to work overseas. The passage comes from early in Jesus' ministry. As soon as he has selected his twelve disciples Jesus calls them together and gives them power and authority to drive out demons and cure diseases. Then he sends them out to preach about the Kingdom of God and heal the sick; they are to take no extra staff, bag, food, no money, not even an extra shirt (Luke 9:3). With some significant differences, the words are also there in Matthew and Mark.

Needs and Outcomes

The reason many missionaries choose these words for their departure to another place is obvious – they want to preach the kingdom of God, and heal the people they go to serve, even if they are not the physically sick. They choose it because they feel they are being sent by God, as the disciples were. Many will not want Matthew's version (Matthew. 10.5-16) which tells them to ignore Gentiles and Samaritans (seen to be a ban on converting people of other faiths). I used this text to show that in our modern world the scriptures are just as relevant as ever. That is only true, however, if we discern Jesus' Principles, rather than grasping onto unchangeable rules. Biblical rules were established to deal with whatever was important at that time, but then became much more a show of faith than was intended. Few if any missionaries now take the words literally – 'take nothing but a staff, no bread, no bag, no money' – most of them are more likely to have a four-by-four and a satellite phone. 'Forget the detail', they would say, 'it's the principle that counts'. In modern jargon, 'Look at the outcomes Jesus wanted – tackle the needs of the individuals and their community'. Jesus' words need to connect with our own generation and our own culture. Missionaries are selective and choose to ignore portions of biblical text – solving the problem by looking at Jesus' Principles.

A leading thinker on urban mission and church planting, Stuart Williams, wrote some passages for the Bible Reading Fellowship on the theme 'Mission after Christendom'[1] saying that mission in Britain today is very like the world that the apostles had to deal with at the time Christianity began. Now, as then, in the prevailing culture the Christian story is largely unknown; they were then, and we are now, a minority. We are almost aliens in our own place, just one community in a plural society. I would add that we are challenged by that society - particularly when we seem to argue about detail rather than principle, the literal truth of the Bible rather than Jesus' aims and hopes and the very nature of God whose wisdom underlies all our faith. Many Christians have made the words of the Bible writers more important than the Word, which we claim as the very essence, if not the actual being, of God himself. That understanding of the Word would be behind everything I said in any church, but especially to that London congregation I was part of for over ten years.

Peter learns a new Principle

The best biblical support I use to justify this position is found in chapters 10 and 11 of the Acts of the Apostles – also a much-used story in the farewell services of those going to be involved in mission work. In this we hear of Cornelius who, even though he is from a different faith (would Matthew have

---

[1] Bible Reading Fellowship, Guidelines, May - August 2006, pp. 39ff.

approved?) is told by an angel to fetch Peter, the Jewish apostle, and now an early Christian leader. Meanwhile a hungry Peter, at prayer before his supper, has a vision of a sheet coming down full of foods forbidden to him as a Jew, and he is commanded to kill and eat. First he refuses: *'Certainly not Lord, I have never eaten anything 'ritually unclean or defiled'* (Acts 10:14, GNB). But it happens three times, and the voice tells him that what God has made clean he has no right to call unclean. Then the messengers from Cornelius arrive and Peter puts two and two together. It was a life-changing moment and Peter is able to say, *'I now realize that it is true that God treats everyone on the same basis. Those who fear him and do what is right are acceptable to him, no matter what race they belong to.'* (Acts 10:34-35, GNB). It was an astounding about-face, but at first only in theory. His mind had been changed but his heart needed to change too – and when he was half-way through his first sermon to Cornelius' household the Spirit came on them all (Acts 10:44f) as already on Cornelius himself (Acts 10:30ff). Peter was astounded – no classes and no preparation as we insist on today, they got baptised because they proclaimed the greatness of God.

Now Peter had not been scared to say what he had inherited and thought. He had already remarked that: *'a Jew is not allowed by his religion to visit or associate with Gentiles'* (Acts 10:28, GNB), but he now knew he had to change, and he continued: *'God has shown me that I must not consider any person ritually unclean or defiled'* (Acts 10:28, GNB). There was what we might now call a cultural discomfort. He thought he knew God's rules but realised he was still learning about the real intention of the God whose message he has been busy proclaiming.

In the next bit of the story Peter goes to Jerusalem. He faces criticism – *'You were a guest in the home of uncircumcised Gentiles, and you even ate with them!'* (Acts 11:3, GNB). But Peter tells of his culture-shock, and of the story which changed the emerging Christian world: God spoke to him in a vision; the Spirit instructed him to go; an angel prepared Cornelius; he had only just started speaking when the Spirit came on the Gentiles and God gave them the same gift that had been given to the disciples at Pentecost in Jerusalem.

That story still challenges us today. Our mission, with or without staff, bread, bag, money or whatever, is only going to work if we address the situation before us and accept that there may be new ideas coming from outside our traditions or accepted rules. It is not something we can get around by saying that Peter was right to abandon ancient traditions, because the Old Testament has been replaced by the New. The danger in saying that is in stepping back to where Peter was before his revelation. This can be difficult for those who see the New Testament as having a very different authority from the Old, even as it was understood in Peter's time. I would argue that the same applies now – the New Testament is getting on for two thousand years old. It should be our task to follow the life-changing and momentous example of Peter and wrestle with the implications of what we read in our Holy Scripture. As in Peter's time, God wants us to change. We need to relate to today's culture, while understanding our two-thousand-year-old Scripture and the issues specific texts were then relating to. In using them we need to look at principles and not detailed old rules.

One secular parallel suggested to me was that of 'case law'. This legal construct means that more flexible 'regulations' are established by looking at past decisions and creating new laws, which can themselves be changed, modified, or even rescinded. Precedents are important but may be ignored if seen to be dated. I am not sure if this is a true or helpful parallel, as there might be a risk of reinforcing past decisions rather than looking more deeply at the foundation on which decisions should always be based. An example of this difficulty is in the conflicting views on women's ministry. Looking at any 'cases' within the Roman Catholic Church would show no change in theory or practice: Jesus appointed only men as Apostles, so only men can become priests. Some Evangelicals would agree, though preferring 'minister' to 'priest'. Is this a principle, or just a matter of first century culture? Jesus was certainly liberal towards women, so why no female Apostles? The argument is once again dividing the Anglican Church. Are there clues that can help to resolve this?

Jesus and old Rules

Jesus was versed in Jewish law which, in some cases, he saw as no longer relevant even if once it was. But he also went back to some simple basics, quoting Leviticus 19:18 – *'Love your neighbour as yourself'* (NRSV). Luke's version of Jesus' response to questions about important laws has this quote immediately followed by an illustration, perhaps the best-known of his stories – the Parable of the Good Samaritan (Luke 10:25-28 and 29-37).

One difficult issue for Christians who accept that not all scripture has equal authority today is deciding what should be adapted to modern times. If just one rule or custom is ignored, have we undermined belief in the very Word of God? Ignoring what Jesus did to some of the old rules and customs, there is a view that the rejection of any verse in the Bible would mean nothing could be given the reverence it now has. Abandon one and the rest are vulnerable – where do you draw the line? Christian groups that will not wear clothes with zips because they are not mentioned in the Bible have chosen a line that sounds silly to most of us, almost a double negative. But, again, where do we draw the line?

Many people would start from the other end – there are specific things which are clearly forbidden. Many of the Old Testament commands and customs are now irrelevant to the world we live in; indeed, some may appear embarrassing, out-and-out wrong, or just downright silly: you would not be able to approach the altar if you had an eyesight problem, for example, and I wear glasses, so I should never do that. There are much more serious examples which Jesus himself dealt with, and the classic one comes just before the commissioning of disciples that we began with. This is the well-known story of the woman who had a haemorrhage; if we still kept Biblical rules she would not have been allowed into any church for the past twelve years (Luke 8:43-47). Such rules were part of the general discrimination against women allowed in scripture – in early Biblical times you could sell your own daughter into slavery, and even in court a man's testimony would always count for more than a woman's. Christians now see such physical abuse and discrimination as unacceptable, though even in the New Testament slavery was still accepted. Not everything has changed – the world's largest Christian body still discriminates against women in terms of ministry and, some will claim, in issues such as abortion. The Church would have become very different from the rule-dominated Judaism it sprang from if Peter's mission was successful in making everyone understand the need for change. And that's important for us to get hold of – our church growth, our mission in Britain, may now have stagnated because we have not followed those early leaders and made changes to meet a new world. Maybe we need to test the boundaries as they did.

So let's take Peter's example further. As a Jew he would not eat certain foods, but he was given a vision of lots of different foods and came to see that the rules he was used to were to do with his history and culture. At the time, of course the food rules made sense. Pork, for example, was very sensibly forbidden to Jews – before the advent of fridges, pork, in that climate, could easily cause food poisoning and so was a dangerous meat to have around. Common sense became a religious rule because they believed God wanted the best for all people. In that cultural decision, community sense, tradition and religion were all combined. Perhaps we should today establish a new tradition of faith-based community values around fair trade shopping and environmentally-sensitive farming.

The challenge today

So, in terms of cultural change for us today, what is the most challenging? Historically, probably the major change from the Old Testament is not to do with personal relationships, but money. Jesus seemed to target the wealthy as the real sinners – probably still true today for nations as well as for individuals – but what church would stop a millionaire from giving their 10% tithe to church funds? Declare them a sinner? No! Give us your money! We disapprove of gambling, but are mainly happy to accept Lottery winnings. But in the Old Testament our whole business system was not allowed – it was forbidden to take interest on a loan (Islam has a similar ban). In pointing out how we can be selective in what we choose to modify from the Old Testament an article on the Gay and Lesbian Christian Movement (LGCM) website suggests,

> *Usury is condemned quite as fiercely as sodomy and yet today almost everybody has a bank account without feeling that they are breaking some fundamental moral law.* [2]

Sadly, some Jews abused the Principle that one should not take advantage of others; they kept the rules within their own faith, but felt able to loan money to people of other faiths - one of the later sources of anti-Semitism. But to return to the LGCM article,

> *With the growth of capitalist mercantile economies, with their huge demand for venture capital, in the Europe of the Renaissance, pressure was put on the church also to relax the rules. The church found it convenient to go along with this and the rule was dropped. Biblical writers would be appalled but we take banking entirely for granted.*

(This was written before the financial crisis of 2008 – should Christians now be working to re-establish the Old Testament position?)

Three Guidelines

The LGCM article also looks at war, slavery, women and the concept of hell, and ends by looking at three guidelines for biblical authority today. First, as Jesus himself rejected much

---

[2] 'Usury' in 'Difference is not a sin', in 'But the Bible…', Neil Dawson, www.lgcm.org.uk

of the tradition in which he was brought up, so we should act in the same way: *'His was an ethic of principle rather than an ethic of rules'*. Second, our knowledge and understanding of the world has grown as well. It quotes Bishop Spong of Newark, who describes how in mediaeval times the church used the bible to condemn Copernicus, who said the earth was no longer the centre of the universe. The Church has continued to lose credibility against scientific knowledge. Thirdly, we need to understand natural law, otherwise described as *'the perfect law of God'*, which can never be perfectly achieved. *'We have our God-given intelligence to look at and to think about our world'*. From this we can decide what we should and should not believe. The church should be there to give people the tools to come to decisions – and then to act.

Back to a Sermon

I began by thinking of an old sermon, and I will get to it, but before that two important clarifications. As the next chapter will show, the Principles are not selective Church rules. They are moral guidelines based on the words of the most highly regarded person the world has known. But to have wider appeal, including to myself, they do not need to be tied to any essential religious belief. Our faith is in the person and his words but is not dependent on his origin or final achievement.

This is hard for many Christians. The idea that moral Principles can only come from God is one I would not argue against, but I am wary of theology and doctrine taking over. Christian theology endeavours to establish who and what Jesus was. Jesus' own 'being', rather than behaviour, is therefore central to a great many Christians. Actions are of secondary importance and are often strongly influenced by doctrines or even 'ordinances' – the latter being a kind of authoritative direction for people to follow. Any organisation has to have membership rules to be followed but, once again, these are not Principles. For people of many faiths the love of God is central – if God is love then followers should aspire to love him, their neighbours, and the whole of creation. This gives Christians added impetus to find the right way to behave.

Concentrate on Principles

But I prefer to concentrate on Principles for three reasons:

First, it can enable those of less certain faith to seek more faith by keeping scripture and Jesus at the core of their lives.

Second, it could involve people of no faith who may presently have negative or distorted views of Christianity.

Third, it gives freedom to those who question major doctrines as analysed by Church leaders (this is explored in Chapter 11 on 'Human Embryology').

For these three groups of people, Principles can reveal new meaning and understanding of Jesus as well as some guidelines. For more conventional Christians the idea hopefully encourages wider thinking. This is my intention for them – not to denigrate or challenge. In one sense I admire and envy those with certain faith, hoping I might be wrong in my lack of belief in an after-life (this is explored in Chapter 13 on 'Hope'). But I also hope they might look more deeply into where Jesus leads for our personal and global ethics and behaviour.

What I actually said

When I originally gave the sermon on this subject I had not seen the web-based material above and would certainly not have quoted it at such length. Independently coming to the theme of 'Principle or Rule' and having talked about the issue of discrimination against women, this is exactly what I said:

In our own church the issue is something else, and raising this may upset some people – our worldwide church is being divided on homosexuality. Conservative and liberal seem to be equally intransigent in their stand on this issue. So let's look at Principle and not detail again. And though this may sound odd, let's go back to those Old Testament food laws. What was the Principle? At a time when there was no division between sacred and secular, common sense (about not eating pork) became a religious rule to help the community survive.

*So what about homosexuality? Why was it spoken against - though I think only six times in the Old Testament and only once in the New and never mentioned at all by Jesus? Why was it condemned? On the same principle it must have something to do with the community God wanted. Well, think of that world. Most children dying before the age of five, many women dying in childbirth, if your brother died it was a man's job to give the widow children. In other words for the family, the clan, the tribe to survive **everyone** had to be part of the process. It would weaken that poor survival rate even more if someone opted out because of their sexuality. There would be no-one to look after the old, not enough potential adults to hunt or grow food – the family, the clan, the tribe would die. The rule may then have been right, but now that argument makes no sense.*

We live largely as single family units, we have medical services, and we have too many people in the world. The rule was right for its time, but what makes it right now? If we have abandoned other customs of the Old Testament, why not those few about homosexuality too? Our community is in fact strengthened by gay people – who are much more likely to be working in health and education, and indeed as priests. God told Peter he should not call anyone profane or unclean. If we're following ancient customs and law, should we bring back slavery, should we allow the ethnic cleansing God seems to approve of in Exodus 34 – or the abuse of children that our current laws would have us in court for? If we followed those biblical rules and culture, no women here could be on the electoral roll, let alone be on the PCC, and certainly not become a churchwarden or a priest, or indeed a bishop, as our national synod agreed yesterday was theologically acceptable. The argument against was that Jesus didn't have any female apostles. That's true, he worked within his culture, but where it was possible he changed things. He healed on the Sabbath, he ate and drank with people seen as sinners, talked to, learned from, touched and healed women and non-Jews, physically threw people out of the Temple, and so much more. He didn't see God's revelation as limited to early Jewish laws. Through him God revealed so much to us of a possible future, and God's promised Spirit urges us to do even more.

So what about today's gospel? Go out, two by two, take nothing with you. I think it applies to us. Jesus wasn't talking about foreign mission. Preach, heal and combat evil, said Jesus. Tell and demonstrate something simple and new, a message that relates to your neighbours. He was talking about the village next door; for us, Camberwell, Nunhead, Bermondsey. Peter did the same, he adjusted his message to the people he was with, people who had little to start from. So **we** have to do the same, address the issues we face now and understand that the gospel message should transcend, should cancel out, all human-imposed divisions. We should become an even more diverse and loving community and we will find that our message will intrigue people who have never really heard it before.

Mission is from everywhere to everywhere, so let those missionaries who choose today's gospel as their inspiration go to wherever they are going, not restricted by commands about how many pairs of sandals they are allowed, but motivated by the Principle that what they do is more important than their personal state. Preach, heal and combat evil. God's overriding hope is that all people should learn of his love and that **that** should be above and behind and below and surround everything we do. Look beyond the detail, remember the principles. Get out there and do it - preach, heal and combat evil.

Principles rather than rules – but beyond preaching, healing and combating evil (however widely we interpret those) how do we discover the Principles? We should start with Jesus' words. We need to go Back to the Beginning.

CHAPTER 8

Back to the Beginning

Memory is a strange thing. Words and names have always been a problem for me and I am much more into pictures. As part of remembering together the wonderful twelve years we have shared, Gaby is turning the pages of our photo albums and reading the diaries written on holidays. She remembers names and I remember what happened next. If describing how to get somewhere, Gaby would know the street names, I would know to turn left at the monkey puzzle tree. She is good at languages and accents, with Italians in restaurants often thinking she is one of them. Learning languages has always been hard for me – at school it was suggested I took woodwork rather than French at 'O' level because my vocabulary was almost non-existent.

About two years before my MND diagnosis I began to find difficulties with ordinary words, even forgetting the word 'apron' when I needed one at the kitchen sink. We tried crosswords and IQ puzzles to try to keep my brain active in that way but it seemed to make little difference. Later, I helped with some research into MND which showed I had above-average scores on most tests (such as predicting the next item in a sequence) but did badly in giving names to pictures of everyday objects. One theory is that memory problems are linked to MND, and even that from such problems it might be possible to predict the diagnosis – but, if this is right, it will take a long time to prove and until a treatment is discovered it will have no effect on the progress of the disease. Memory is also an 'age thing'. People who have passed their sixtieth birthday (like me and probably St. Mark when he wrote his gospel) are often said to be better at remembering their childhood than what happened yesterday.

Perhaps for some people, including me, that may be partly to do with their enjoyment of life as well as decline in brain cells. 'Djona ve ya Kalunga, O ho kufa po omatimba onyeni, tu pa ombili yoyeh.' Undoubtedly that is spelt wrongly but, apart from the greeting as we passed one another – which also included 'ombili' (peace) - that is all I remember of Oshikwanyama, the language of a large group within the Ovambo people of northern Namibia and southern Angola. I was there for a year nearly forty years ago. We sang those words at the main Sunday service every week –O Lamb of God (Kalunga) who takes away the sins of the world, grant us your peace.

I remember reading bedtime stories to my son. He would appear to be asleep, so I would skip or abbreviate a page. If I did that he would suddenly sit up and quote the piece I had missed. He was not in the culture or time discussed below. In one sense he was demonstrating something that happened in biblical times and happens in developing countries today; many people two thousand years ago were illiterate but had memories of the exact content of stories. It is difficult for some people to believe that could have been possible, as our concentration is said to have diminished substantially, yet people still remember the lyrics of the pop songs of their youth.

Mark and Memory

What did Mark remember of Jesus? He would have been looking back roughly the same number of years as I am to my time in Ovamboland. Why did he decide to write his 'good news'? Was it because many of the people who had personal memories of Jesus had died? Or, despite their ability to remember exact words in stories, did he need to correct some of the exaggerated versions going around? Or was it that belief in Jesus was spreading fast but without real knowledge of his life? Probably a mixture of all those. As the earliest of the gospels, his collection of Jesus stories is, for me, the source of the Principles which apply to this age as much as his. We will return to him later.

In my own life the people who influenced me most were connected with my time in southern Africa. Three people were especially important. Only one, Desmond Tutu, is still alive and is one of the few church leaders speaking out on local, international and church issues such as HIV/AIDS. He still shows us all how core beliefs should relate to real life – with Principles, not rules. I have already written in Chapter 5 about Colin Winter and how his preaching related to real life. After his deportation by the South African government, he wrote 'Namibia – the Story of a Bishop in Exile'. In that he quoted Trevor Huddleston, the third of my great heroes, who himself had written back in 1954,

> *The Church sleeps on …. It sleeps on while a dictatorship is swiftly being created … so that speech and movement and association are no longer free. The Church sleeps on – though it occasionally talks in its sleep and expects (or does it?) the government to listen.* [1]

---

[1] Bishop Trevor Huddleston in The Observer 10/08/1954, quoted in Colin Winter (1977) Namibia – The Story of a Bishop in Exile, Lutterworth Press, p. 212

In the same chapter of Colin's book, he wrote of the cost of discipleship in the apartheid era:

> *It is often dangerous to try to live as a genuine Christian. Some Christians there can say with Saint Paul: 'I bear in my body the marks of the Lord Jesus.*

He adds a little later:

> *I salute them; I yearn for the church to stand by them, to see them as the spiritual children of Isaiah, Amos, and Jeremiah.*

When I listen to religious conservatives, who no doubt would have been able to dissect Colin's sermons and writings as much as they oppose the stance of Desmond Tutu, I am reminded of a poem in a book given to me by Bishop Colin:

> *We watched the white man's arrival,*
> *in strange-shaped ships we did not know.*
> *Now we have become trespassers,*
> *on the shores of our land.*
>
> *He brought with him a book,*
> *that spoke of a new religion.*
> *Of love, humility and compassion,*
> *to blind us to his deception.* [2]

---

[2] James David Matthews (1972) Cry Rage! Spro-cas Publications, Bloemfontein, South Africa, p. 5

It is plain to me that these three inspiring leaders were drawing not just on the prophets but on the core teaching of Jesus. That was deep inside them. I call these the Principles of the one we should follow. But where are the Principles to be found? How do we determine what they are? For me, the only way is to go back to the real Jesus and find out what he believed and said, and crystallise what he meant us to do rather than argue about who he was or what happened at his birth or after his death.

Doctrine and reality

I first began this personal search after a Gospel reading just before Christmas in the church I used to attend in London. It highlighted for me something which has always disturbed me - the way the church's concentration on irrelevant doctrinal issues and organisational matters has swamped what the reality of the story of Jesus should be for us today.

The Gospel reading was the foretelling of the birth of Jesus. Despite his obvious aim to engage a Jewish audience, St. Matthew chose a Greek translation of Isaiah to foretell the birth of the ruler of Judah from a 'virgin'. But the Hebrew version says 'a young woman' (Matthew 1:23 and Isaiah 7:14). Modern translations such as the Good News Bible recognise this in their notes. In cultural terms there may not then have been much difference in the two descriptions – some claim they were then synonymous. Matthew's story certainly suggests that Mary had had no sexual relationship with Joseph and presumably with no other man. For that era and culture, whether for the shame or the ridicule it would have meant for him, many see Joseph as unusually generous in being willing to keep quiet. That often-ignored part of the story is as important to the development of church doctrine as the angel Gabriel's announcement of the child who was to be born. In Jewish tradition and law the evidence of a man was supremely important – there would have been no point in Mary herself saying she had conceived as a virgin.

But the idea of virginity had even more importance. Who would believe this was the Son of God if his mother had ever had sexual relationships with an earthly man? Matthew was writing probably at least two generations after the life of Jesus and doctrinal truth had become important. That much is understandable, but what has developed from Matthew's choice of words is perhaps the best example of the move from an event in Jesus' life to a theological doctrine. Historically, doctrine developed partly from a need to prevent schism, but was also to do with retaining authority, with controlling belief and with male dominance.

The teaching today within the world's largest church is that Mary herself was so pure that, like Jesus, she was born free of sin and, like Jesus, ascended or was 'assumed' into heaven. The first mentions of the Assumption are probably fourth century and some versions have it happening, like the Resurrection of Jesus, three days after her death. Other versions mention three days or forty days after the Ascension of Jesus himself. The doctrine was not official in the Roman Catholic Church until 1950 and is widely held in the Orthodox tradition too. The Immaculate Conception became official doctrine nearly one hundred years earlier, after centuries of debate about the meaning of original sin. This included debate on whether sexual intercourse – even between married people – was a sinful act, though pardoned by God. Another question was whether it was a greater redemptive act of God to preserve Mary from original sin than to allow her to be born in the normal way and then be raised above it. Part of this debate asked whether Mary were to be revered as the 'Mother of God', and how this related to the Holy Trinity, especially in an eternal sense.

From an understandable beginning where Mary has, at the very least, to be seen as 'pure' in order to counter any suggestion that Jesus could be the son of a human father, we have moved to a point where she becomes the very symbol of God, to be honoured seemingly as much as Jesus. In many southern European countries Mary rather than Jesus is the central figure within the array of statues behind the high altar. Within the same tradition, she had no sexual relationship with any man. The 'brothers' of Jesus (Mt: 13:46.) have to be called the 'brethren' with the explanation that, as in many cultures, 'brother' includes people the British would label 'cousin'. Mary is seen to be so pure and special that no human could be considered worthy of touching her.

The problem for me is that if Mary was really born totally pure, was assumed into heaven and had the theological wisdom to proclaim what we call the Magnificat, why do we need the figure of Jesus at all? God had rather selected her in some way. So how many generations back will this divinely engineered purity have to go? It seems unnecessary and absurd.

In the history of the Church, to give legitimacy to the dominance that men want and the resulting exploitation of women, they must be like Mary – as obedient to men as she was to God – conveniently backed up by a perversion of the text that men are the head of the household (Eph 5:23). This flowed naturally from Jewish male-dominated culture in which the male-written scriptures largely ignore the important role of women in Israel's history.[3]

There is an argument that if Mary had borne a child before Jesus it would then be difficult for people to believe that Jesus is the Son of God rather than of a human father. This is understandable, but even that has little real significance. There has been so much debate and theological disagreement on all this, and the point here is not to explore it any further, but to ask how it affects our understanding of Jesus, his life and his Principles. Apart from some questioning of this man that they knew as a child in his home town of Nazareth (Mark 6: 4) and some city rudeness about rural Galilee, there is little mention of his origin in the gospels. It is his lifestyle and his teaching which influence people.

God is too Greek?

Other people have explored the development of theology in great depth and in historical, philosophical and cultural contexts. Keith Ward, now a professor, and whose first-ever lectures as a theological faculty junior staff member I well remember, has particularly explored the philosophical links between Plato and later Christian doctrine. One of his themes, outlined in a lecture at Gresham College, was the development of the idea of the Holy Trinity. He links Plato's ideas with a

---

[3] One of the best deconstructions of the accepted idea of the insignificance of women is expounded by Trevor Dennis in Sarah Laughed, SPCK, 1994, particularly his chapter on Hagar, whose first-hand dealings with God were as significant as those of any man and whose role in Jewish history was, in many ways, as important as that of Abraham.

later thinker, Plotinus, who himself influenced Origen and the decisions of the Council of Constantinople,

> *Platonism provided the concepts in terms of which Christian orthodoxy was defined, and enshrined the Trinitarian nature of God at the heart of its new religion.* [4]

Plato is also seen by Christopher Jamison as the reason for the separation of spirituality from the rest of ourselves.

> *Rather than seeing the spiritual as involving the whole of life, Christians now emphasised the distinction between body and soul…The body/soul distinction became deeply embedded in the European outlook and persists today in the phrase 'a Platonic relationship'. Spirituality became disconnected from the physical and private…The body/soul split was institutionalised and every aspect of life was divided between the temporal and spiritual.* [5]

Jamison, here, is looking at spirituality in general, but begins by pointing out that St. Paul saw Christians as people who have the mind of Christ. To be unspiritual is to be greedy and selfish, not to be 'secular'. To be a genuine Christian was to have the word of Christ dominate all of life.

Robert Hood goes further, using the same historical links as Keith Ward, and entitling his book Must God remain Greek? [6] His argument, too, is that the way we are supposed to think

---

[4] Keith Ward, The Formation of Christian Doctrine, lecture at Gresham College, downloadable from www.gresham.ac.uk.

[5] Christopher Jamison (2006) Finding Sanctuary, Weidenfield & Nicholson, p.140

[6] Robert Hood (1990) Must God Remain Greek?, Fortress Press

about our faith has been dominated by the narrow thought-world of Greece and Rome. The system which controls this thought (theologians, bishops, councils and liturgists) have a stranglehold, determining what is orthodox and acceptable.

Theology, history and culture

Theologians from the developing world see doctrine influenced by the dominant western culture. This is obvious in traditional Christian art, in which Jesus is a blue-eyed, white-skinned western European, still seen in churches across the world. Stanley Samartha, who was both the first director of the World Council of Churches Dialogue Programme and a Professor at the United Theological College in Bangalore, points out that none of the biblical events took place in the native context of these dominant western theologians. However accurate we believe translation to be, the words we read come to us, in the case of Jesus, from Aramaic, through Greek, into English. Basic concepts such as 'love' and 'fatherhood' have different nuances in different cultures and the same is true of demon possession, miracles and health issues, and the position of women. The verb 'to be' does not exist in all languages in the same sense – and sayings of Jesus such as 'This **is** my Blood' can have many interpretations. Even the gender, or the grouping of words (English words in particular since they have no gender), can influence the perceived meaning of phrases. Samartha suggests we should take more notice of those whose thought patterns and way of life are closer to those of the biblical writers. [7]

---

[7] Stanley Samartha (1990) The Holy Spirit and the People of other Faiths, in the Ecumenical Review, vol. 42, nos. 3-4, p.113

Robert Hood writes from his black North American cultural perspective, while Neil Fujita comes to this from a Japanese angle. He sees 'western' Christianity as 'conic'. God, we are to understand, is the top of a monarchical system, in which 'king of kings' would be a typical image. [8] Faith becomes a matter of absolutes – a Greek 'either/or' tradition which is different from the 'both/and' of Japanese thinking.

What I am stressing in these three criticisms – of the development of the doctrine of the Virgin Mary, of the non-Christian Greek foundation of theology and of the way our western culture has influenced the way we believe – is that we have moved away from putting our faith's founder at the centre of everything. What were his priorities? Has modern theology and the twenty-first century Church moved away from these? Was it not Jesus' performance, words and lifestyle which influenced people and, if so, how do we follow these today? Even if the precise details of any of the above criticisms can be disputed, surely the words, example and commands of Jesus – understood in relation to the culture he lived in – must be at the centre of everything. We have no record from the time Jesus was alive, but the stories and events were remembered. It is important for my argument that the earliest Gospel and the earliest Epistle – Mark and James – are seen as the most radical.

James - Validity and Significance

Mark's Gospel was probably written around 65AD, but James's letter may have been as early as 45AD. There is a contrary theory that it was written much later, partly because of the

---

[8] Neil Fujita (1994) Missiology, vol. xxii, no. 1

standard of the Greek text. But in 1.24-25 and 2.8-13 James seems to presume that the Torah is acceptable as Scripture. This suggests it was written before the changes resulting from the Apostolic Council of around 48 or 49 AD. If it was written after that, James might well have grappled with Paul's theology of justification by faith alone. One suggestion for the identity of the author is the brother of Jesus, and this may be a partial explanation for its resemblance to Old Testament prophets, known for their certainty and authority. The epistle is clearly important if there is indeed a close link through family and also because of the likely brief interval since Jesus' preaching had been heard.

James' letter is seen by some as unsystematic and therefore of poorer quality than those of St. Paul. It may also be because the content is too challenging, but mainly because of that conflict with Paul about 'faith'. Paul sees faith as enveloping everything. It is obedience to God which includes right actions. For James, however – and this is why many Christians downgrade, if not ignore, his letter – there appears to be a separation of faith and 'works'. Can it be that Christians just a few generations later, when Paul was writing, had already concluded that doctrinal exactitudes were at least as important as actions? Perhaps James was over-stressing part of the correct combination of elements when he wrote: *'It is by his actions that a person is put right with God, and not by his faith alone'* (James 2:24, GNB). But this is not a denial that faith is an important element, just that faith *without* works (mere 'belief' in a kind of esoteric way) is dead (James 2:17, 20, 24, 26). Luther called it an 'epistle of straw' and was clearly unimpressed, but that may have more to do with his separation of Church and State.

While the James/Paul issue is a tricky one for those who maintain that there is no conflict in the 'truth' of scripture, my issue is to try to discover the writings which are closest to the words of Jesus. Historical proximity and/or relationship are vital.

James is often seen as a 'primitive' Christian text, written for an early, persecuted and mainly Jewish Christian church, probably passed from one synagogue or home to another as groups were considering the significance of Jesus. In that sense it was more a sermon which, just as today, encourages involvement in ethical conduct and life. It also has strong suggestions of an early end to the world which is missing from later texts. The writer has been described as having pastoral concern – a 'street-level theology'. While stressing the need for mutual support to help each other through likely persecution, James emphasizes concern for the poor. Faith is put to work through action.

All these theories and disagreements are significant in establishing the validity of James' Epistle, but it is the content which is important – and more so in my mind because I believe it is the earliest book in the New Testament and therefore close to the real Jesus.

Content is what matters

James's thoughts and warnings are very clear, but he begins and ends with traditional themes around the life of Christians at that time. Christians may have to deal with persecution (1:2-4) and must be confident in holding together God and wisdom (1:5-8). They must have patience in the time of oppression until the Lord comes (5:7-11). They should pray if in trouble and elders will succeed in healing those with faith

(5:13-15). Sins should be confessed and prayer will bring healing (5:16-18) and bringing back a sinner to the right path will save that person's soul (5:19-20).

The major and central part of the letter is about behaviour. It begins with a desire for humility (1:9-11) and a statement that good comes from God and that personal evil desire produces sin and therefore draws people away from God (1:12-18). Then from 1:19 to 5:7 we read how Christians should therefore behave:

1:19-21	Be slow to get angry – this is 'filthy habit and wicked conduct'.
1:22-27	The word of God has to be put into practice as well as listened to.
2:1-13	People do not deserve respect just for their place in society. God chose the poor, but it is the rich who dishonour and oppress them.
2:14-26	Good actions are needed as well as faith.
3:1-12	The tongue is like a fire, it can be evil and uncontrollable.
3:13-18	Wisdom from above is in contrast to envy, jealousy, bitterness and selfishness. Goodness is the harvest from the seeds planted by peacemakers.
4:1-3	Violence comes from greed and desire for pleasure.
4:4-10	Pride is one of the results of being the world's friend (i.e. concerned with yourself – this is not anti-conservation as some have inferred!)
4:11-12	Be careful not to criticise others.
4:13-16	Business confidence is vain and concerned only with this world.

5:1-6	A warning to the rich, especially those who have exploited their employees; those full of luxury and pleasure who have killed the innocent.

Despite our huge cultural differences and the nearly two thousand years since James was writing, it is not difficult to relate his words to today. Do not those who exploit the poor in the developing world, using child labour, unsafe working conditions and minimal wages fit easily into the beginning of chapter 5 and early chapter 2? Does not violence and associated greed link with the turmoil in so many countries? How many of us are so concerned with being the world's friends (trends in everything from fashion to choice of job, or even politics) that selfish pride is more important for us than anything else? It would be easy to link many of his passages with the financial crisis in the early years of the twenty-first century.

Mark's Gospel – the real thoughts of Jesus

James' main themes are also found in the earliest and shortest of the four gospels accepted into the Canon of the Bible. Mark gives no account of the birth or early years of Jesus. If we accept the date of around 65AD, then few of those who had been with or directly experienced Jesus in some way would still be around; but in that largely pre-literate era, people would have a memory for stories. This does not mean that Mark's Gospel is not a carefully engineered and chosen set of stories. However, if we accept both the early date and the argument that later Christians preferred and therefore selected doctrines, ideas and texts more suited to their own ideas, thoughts and situation, then it has to be seen as the closest to the words and life of Jesus. Both Matthew and Luke added birth and early years' stories and expanded on Mark's shorter texts. They also chose to change some of the text, omitting or modifying text or adding extra material to present a more easily acceptable view of the words and actions of Jesus.

Story, Response and Initiative

The Gospel's first sentence lets readers or listeners know who the stories are about – Jesus is the Christ, the Son of God, the centre of all that is to come. Looking at the gospel as a whole, there are three different categories of content: *story, response* and *initiative*. But what emerges, especially from *response* and *initiative* are three Principles which I see as key to how his followers should conduct their lives today.

Large sections of Mark's Gospel can be labelled as *story*. By *story* I mean descriptions of events, some of which may have doctrinal importance (e.g. the fact of crucifixion).The largest *story* section is the last three chapters (14-16) which deal with Jesus' arrest, trial, crucifixion and resurrection. Other *story* sections include the calming of the storm (4:35-41); Jesus' rejection by his home village (6:1-6); Herod's view that he is a re-born John the Baptist (6:14-29); walking on water (6:45-52); the account of a number of healings in Gennesaret (6:53-56); and the beginning section about John the Baptist, Jesus' Baptism and Temptation.

There are further sections which are part of the larger 'story' where Jesus either *responds* to particular situations with comments or thoughts, or *initiates* through action or comment. It is in these sections that we see Jesus' Principles.

Establishing the Principles

The first two chapters are a good example, clearly intended to establish the authority and also the person and power of Jesus. Apart from the calling of the disciples and the early authority-establishing healing miracles (1:21-28; 29-34; 40-45; 2:1-12), Jesus' first recorded action in Mark's version is to pray and preach (1:35-39). The next action is within a very mixed account of *response* to others. His own initiative is to eat with sinners - his call is to outcasts since it is the sick who need a doctor (2:15-17). Then fasting is challenged because this is a new and special time, like a wedding (2:18-20). This is followed immediately by 'newness'; old coats can't be repaired with new cloth and new wine needs new wineskins (2:21-22). Even sin is dealt with very differently from the accepted ideas of the rule-following rich. It is still sin, but it is as if those with less status are understood more and blamed less.

All this establishes early on the Principles which Jesus follows up in his later actions and words:

- no-one is excluded,
- the vulnerable and outcast need more help than others – despite and perhaps because they are led to sin, and,
- the old ways are not good enough. [9]

---

[9] The Beatitudes in Matthew's Gospel are shorthand statements about important ways in which these Principles have been suggested to us. 'Blessed are the peacemakers' is explored in 'Peace', available as a download from www.GileadBooksPublishing.com. But peace in this sense only has value if it upholds the vulnerable and outcast, and if no-one is excluded. The 'trickledown theory' that increasing wealth for a minority will also benefit the poor has certainly been supported by many, including some Christians, but high amounts of retained

These ideas are not confined to that early section of Mark. The central section of the Gospel is again a mixture of *story*, *response*, and *initiative.* The *response* and *initiative* elements predominate, and show us the teaching of Jesus alongside the proof of his authority in successful healing and some preaching.

Chapter three is especially important in affirming the Principles which Jesus demonstrated and which the first chapters expounded: no-one excluded; the vulnerable need help; old ways are not good enough. Following the criticism of the disciples for plucking wheat on the Sabbath and the response that the Sabbath was made for the good of humankind (2:23-27) comes a healing on the Sabbath (3:1-6) – because life-saving is more important than petty rules. Here Jesus is both angry about and sorry for his critics. Then there are two sections relating to Jesus' family. They want to take charge of him because he is seen by some as being mad. Jesus' response is to talk about unity and fighting evil by working together (3:20-27). Strength comes from being united. The family then call him and Jesus proclaims that those who do God's will are the real family – a new kind of unity.

The next group of healing stories and parables (4:1-6:56) has two main *initiatives* from Jesus – the sending out of the disciples with very few resources (6:7-13) and his concern for

---

personal income surely conflict with the Principles. The financial crisis which began in 2008 was triggered by greed overcoming common sense (in Chapter 2 I explore this further, looking at recent research which suggests that within the developed economies, the greater the difference between richest and poorest the more there are problems in everything from violence to education).

the vulnerable (if also negligent and unprepared) in the feeding of the five thousand (6:30-44).

The Pharisees then attack Jesus for not washing hands before eating. This gives Jesus an opportunity to counter-attack by accusing them of amending family rules so that people's needy parents are disadvantaged (7:1-13). Again, the old ways are condemned. Immediately following is Jesus own list of what is really undesirable activity – robbery, killing, adultery, greed, deceit, indecency, jealousy, slander, pride and folly (7:14-23). Whether in any particular sequence or not, we are given the list of evils – and then Jesus is himself challenged about another evil.

The challenge comes from a Gentile woman, and what follows is a key *response* to the woman who challenges what, in modern terms, is a mixture of racism (or at least ethnic/tribal preference) and gender discrimination (7:24-30). Some Christians are reluctant to admit that here the 'perfect' Jesus shows he can learn too, while many feel that describing a group of people as 'dogs', even if they are to get the crumbs under the table, hardly does him credit. Some also point out that the word 'dog' was not then as derogatory as it is now. But again, the outcome benefits the vulnerable – in this case a woman whose race and faith are not acceptable in Jewish society, and whose need leads to Jesus changing the old rules.

My analysis moves now to the final chapters (but there is similar analysis of other chapters in appendix A). Within the 'Passion' story there are again three important *initiatives* by Jesus – the overturning of the Temple tables (11:15-19); the lesson to the lawyer that the powerful abuse the poor and therefore damage their own status (12:7b-40); and the parable of the tenants who kill all who come, including the owner's son. It is obviously a parable about himself but, just as the widow's mite tells of his own self-sacrifice, so this could remind those who follow Jesus' ethical Principles that they too have to behave properly in relating to both rich and poor.

As in the very first section, vulnerability, need and newness are major themes. What we have revealed to us in Mark's Gospel, through Jesus' use of *story, response* and *initiative* when faced with challenges, situations and specific questions, is in reality a very simple list of the ways we should behave if we wish to follow the man and his ideals rather than developed doctrines about his person (or, as this chapter began, about his mother!). Jesus' three Principles are demonstrated in caring for others, working together to strengthen unity that advances all, self-sacrifice rather than wealth-accumulation, ending the abuse of the poor, and eschewing self-aggrandisement. Mark's record of the work and words of Jesus excludes any selfish hope for salvation.

Mark's gospel clearly means a great deal to theologians who come from poor communities, thirty-three of whom contributed chapters to the book Voices from the Margin – sub-titled Interpreting the Bible in the Third World. [10] Of the gospel quotations they use, 119 come from Mark, but only 145 from all the other three Gospel writers.

Ethics, Behaviour and Principles

Resurrection and ascension are fundamental to almost all who call themselves Christian but are a matter of faith; neither can be proved though, of course, there are many who claim visions or other proofs. The earliest Epistle and Gospel are much less

---

[10] R.S. Sugitharajah (1991) Voices from the Margin, SPCK

concerned with resurrection and ascension. It is understandable that in later years people would want to know more of Jesus' life, in particular his origin and end, but the central theme of the earlier books is thereby reduced. James and Mark are not the only New Testament writers with a concern for 'good works'; of the later writers, St Luke is hugely important. But I have chosen the two early writers because I see in them a closer connection to the founder of the faith which so many people now define as being about personal salvation. They emphasise issues which have an obvious link with the sentiments and pronouncements of the person we are supposed to follow. Though Biblical writers do not have a systematic code of ethics, many church leaders refer to specific texts in scripture as if this was the case. It is as if verse 27 of chapter 23 of book X has the same legal significance as definition 33 (b) of section 497 on page 1156 of government legislation.

From Mark we receive something different. While the *story* element fits the expectations of first century and later believers, we discover in the *response* and *initiative* elements the true Jesus in a wider and much more eternal sense. Shown in a different way also in James, without picking one set of words in preference to others, we have an overall set of Principles around which we should base our action in this and every century. No true believer or follower should put the composed *story* element at a higher level, even if they believe it to be literally true. For Jesus, no-one is excluded, the vulnerable and outcast need more help than others – despite and perhaps because they are led to sin. Statistics show that in the United Kingdom, prisons are full of the poor in many senses – education, mental health, family breakup, etc. Meanwhile, what is known as 'white collar' crime is often kept away from public attention in case the reputation of the company is damaged, though frequently it causes more harm to the community than the often petty crime of the poor.

The old ways are not good enough. An application of these Principles to current debates, national and international politics and community affairs would change everything from individual behaviour to international disputes. It would be naive to think this is simple, but Christians should at least be trying the strategy within their internal disputes.

There is much else in early scripture, including Jesus' explanation of his own person. But was it just his claim of being the Messiah which led to his arrest and crucifixion? There were many other claimants to personal divine links, as there are still today, but what most alienated his opponents was his re-interpretation of their rules, which was also an attack on their power and authority. The question for me is why so many church leaders seem to have the same blind spot, preferring to detail rules which relate to a specific time and culture rather than the Principles of Jesus.

CHAPTER 9

Community and Exclusion

Personal memories

I grew up in Southampton immediately after the Second World War. No-one in our street had a car – the only one that ever came was the doctor's – and we played cricket on the road (six and out if the ball went into a neighbour's garden). There was plenty of unused land around, some cleared following enemy action, other places just not developed in the way that they would be now. One favourite area for games, as well as catching tadpoles and newts and sticklebacks, was a marshy area full of ponds created by bomb craters – the result of targeting a nearby Spitfire factory. We walked there, played all day and returned safely home. Horses were left to feed there; scout groups used it for day and night games.

Now it has been filled in, 'made safe' and is a boring park. But in the real sense of being safe, things have changed. Children do not go there on their own. Streets have more traffic, but that's not the reason; society is now obsessed with health and safety. Parents as well as organised groups would feel it extremely risky to let five year olds go there without direct and close supervision. We are frightened of abusers, accidents, and being sued for lack of responsibility. Liability and fear have taken much of the fun out of childhood; most children today do not play in the way that I did. Adults will think twice about touching a child who has fallen over (as I often did). Something about being together and also reacting to each other has all but gone.

Today's world and Isaiah's vision

My memories represent some of the changes we have become used to – changes in 'community'. As the news constantly reminds us, conflict continues to erupt between nations, tribes, religious groups and communities. In 2009 and 2010 Pakistan and Iraq suffered enormous casualties from radical Islamist suicide bombers unhappy with their governments; this country's public and media counted the number of British troops killed in Afghanistan, in part due to internal divisions; Somalia and Yemen continued also with their internal divisions, and weak governments – one resulting in piracy, the other in terrorism. Zimbabwe continued to be divided on party lines, fundamentally tribal-based. Probably the most divisive on faith grounds was the over-reactive Israeli response to Hamas in Gaza and the continued building of settlements in Palestine, with electricity and water often unavailable to non-Jews, whose land had been stolen. The inability to deal with climate change shows that many political leaders and those who elect them do not see the world as one community.

It all makes me think of that wonderful piece in Isaiah on the Peaceful Kingdom (Isaiah 11:1-9), which imagines for us a community in which previous hostilities disappear. From those verses the part that enlivens my imagination is the idea of cows and bears eating together, lions eating straw with oxen, and babies playing with poisonous snakes. For the rural-living people of Isaiah's time this is a wonderful illustration of the preceding verses about the behaviour of leaders and the principles under which rulers should operate so that societies can flourish.

The United Kingdom is not absent from any community-problems list, and is nowhere near Isaiah's vision. It is divided in so many ways, including hostility by many towards Muslim groups and immigrants. There are many examples of an underlying lack of respect for each other. At the root is often a simple lack of knowledge, obvious in the two places I have most recently lived. Here in Somerset it is often wrongly assumed that we left inner-city London because of racial problems, crime and violence. Meanwhile in Peckham there was surprise that in a small town and nearby villages we have supermarkets, a cinema showing the latest films, the current holder of the 'best fish shop in the UK' award and healthcare easily matching that in cities.

Despite much more travel and availability of information, we seem to know little about each other and in some cases have little thought for each other. Our worlds have become much more private, and the balance between personal rights and feeling for community seems to have changed. Even as tourists, so many people are cocooned in a replica of their home culture and make few links with host communities – we travel in what have been called 'mobile ghettos'. This compartmentalising of our world leads to intolerance of differences which can have disturbing consequences. The separation of personal from community is obvious at every level; we *withdraw into bunkers of the like-minded, vacating the territory of solidarity and common purpose'.* [1] We fail to take seriously Isaiah's wonderful vision of community.

There are serious things happening in the UK which stem from a lack of ability to accept difference, and the insistence of many on their personal rights and preferences. A particularly glaring example is urban youth violence, so often reported in places such as Peckham. There we had the terrible killing of the ten-year old schoolboy Damilola Taylor, who bled to death

---

[1] Madeline Bunting, The Guardian, 28/01/08

after being stabbed with a broken bottle. Then a woman was shot holding a baby at a christening party. In one week in 2007 a fifteen year old boy was shot in his bed, less than a mile away a man was shot dead and another seriously injured, and in a separate incident a man was stabbed to death.

The new poor?

When that fifteen year old boy was killed I listened to a social worker being interviewed on the radio. He said that the problem was the lack of relationships – a new kind of poverty. It came to me that the Gospel had something very important to say to us for our present time. The next day a radio report about posh new housing estates spoke of no space for community, assuming that everyone would get out of their houses and move around by car and have no relationships with any neighbour. We are encouraging poverty of relationships at all levels – while poverty in terms of income and resources is important, relationship-poverty cuts deeper. It reminded me of something said to me by a teacher in another urban area:

> *The only place where children now speak to an adult is in school – and I have 30 of them. At home they either all watch TV together and don't talk or go their separate ways to watch their own in their bedrooms, or play games on computers or spend the evening texting or online. They don't do things together as a family. They don't eat together, they don't talk, they don't play, and when younger they don't have bed-time stories. They don't know how to relate. No-one teaches right and wrong. In one sense families don't exist.*

George M. Soares-Prabhu,[2] who teaches theology in India, maintains that the poor whom Jesus spoke to and about were destitute because of prevailing social conditions, including exploitation by religious leaders. Jesus also supported the illiterate, the socially outcast, the physically disabled, and the mentally ill. All these are victims, and are reduced to *'a condition of diminished capacity or worth'* (p.156). Soares-Prabhu adds that in both Old and New Testaments the poor are also a dynamic group who are bearers of salvation and hope. In what some might see as a classic socialist parallel, Jesus gives up the security of home supported by a locally - needed artisan skill. First followers are other artisans (fishermen), an 'untouchable' tax collector, and an outlawed zealot, probably from a guerrilla group. Zaccheus is possibly the only 'rich' person to give support. Many tax collectors were forced into that despised position because there was no other choice. They were often slaves. Unlike Sadducees, most Pharisees were also lower class, influential because of their piety. Soares-Prabhu then points out (pp.164-5) that the three wealthy followers are not portrayed well: the rich landowner will not sell up to follow Jesus (Mk. 10:17-22); Nicodemus does not want to lose his reputation so only visits at night (John 3:1); and Joseph of Arimathaea (a 'seeker' and not a follower) only helps out at the burial (Mk. 15:43). Soares-Prabhu continues: *'The new humanity, and the communities through which it takes shape, grow through conflict'.* The conflict is resolved *'by an act of God in favour of the poor'*, the coming of Jesus. He ends by saying, *'Salvation comes from God,*

---

[2] George M Soares-Prabhu (1991) Class in the Bible: the Biblical Poor a Social Class?, in Voices from the Margin, ed. R. S. Sugithrarajah, SPCK

but it is actualised in and through the struggles of the poor'
(p.166).

Blessed are the poor

So how do the words of Jesus – 'Blessed are the poor' – apply
to those weaknesses in community we have all witnessed and
which Peckham has felt as much as anywhere else? Jesus knew
the poor. He knew that they helped each other, that they lived
in households, and he knew that these were units, not
collections of individuals thinking only of themselves. He knew
they needed each other, and that poor households rely on
relationships to survive. Relationships are more important
than money because when anything goes wrong, there are
others to help out. So maybe our problem is that we have
effectively lost all that, and with it the trust, the affection, the
ability to sort out problems within communities and families.
Our rules of life are learned in the home, but in the 'civilised'
West we are now into the second generation at least of people
whose lives are dominated by that screen in the corner or on
the wall, if not in every bedroom. So we have parents who
themselves did not experience much in the way of
relationships - which in simple terms means spending time
with each other. Now there is even more opportunity to have
private time – it seems we no longer know how to be in
families and communities.

There is a growing gap between the powerful wealthy and
the poor in our own society, and also the growth of 'celebrity
status' which has little to do with moral values. In some of our
urban estates this is seen in the gang status. An 'ASBO' gives
status. Power and status of the group bring together the wants
of individuals in a way they believe they can be met. When this

is challenged by an individual or another group, violence seems to be the all-too-common resolution.

I believe this is something that many of our teachers and social workers and, where they exist, youth workers would say. But Jesus somehow had it right long ago. He knew that the really poor, who need and often have those trusting relationships, are truly blessed because they reflect the vision God has for his people – they have each other, often rely on each other, and at the same time have in their lives a picture of what real wealth is too. Real wealth is relationships, friends and supporters, affection, sharing of ideas and feelings and exchange of things that are needed by individuals. Soares-Prabhu spoke of communities growing through conflict and that can happen because all begin to see the need for common aims. This is the way in which the poor are truly blessed, which in reality means to be chosen, to be favoured by God in some way.

That might almost seem to be an excuse for the powerful decision-makers to avoid doing anything about physical poverty. 'Let them do it – God has blessed them so they are better off than us,' and sometimes neither government/local authority nor church solutions will work. But if we go back to those words of Isaiah, we have the vision of a ruler with wisdom as well as the knowledge and skill to lead. Neither appearance nor hearsay will influence judgement because the poor will be judged fairly and their rights defended. All will be ruled with justice and integrity. Above all, anyone making the rules for how our society should be, will not only understand the ethical demands of the God they serve, but *will delight in the fear of the Lord. He will not judge by what he sees with his eyes, or decide by what he hears with his ears; but with righteousness he will judge the needy, with justice he will give decisions for the poor of the earth'* (Isaiah 11:3f, NRSV). Examples of the kind of people who followed that vision and of whom we need more today include Tutu and Winter, quoted earlier in 'Back to the Beginning'. The predominant concern for them is for community which has to include all.

Returning to the disciples, the first followers of Jesus, the ones we know about were four fishermen, the untouchable tax collector who gave it all up and the zealot who was a member of an outlawed group – all people despised by others. The equivalents today might be migrant workers, someone hated as a debt collector and maybe a gang leader on one of our estates. But they made a relationship with Jesus, they followed, and in one sense became a community – and they founded our church. True, they let him down at times, especially at the cross. Would we not have run away too? But they did give up everything for him.

God is not telling us it is better to be poor like them in a physical sense. He is telling us that we must think carefully about how much anything we do is self-centred, whether in the way we treat the environment, the domination we enjoy as nations or races or through gender, the wealth we accumulate, or above all our relationships with other people. These can all draw us away from God because our selfishness means we care more about ourselves and less about those around. And those around us are the fruit of God's creation; they are the closest we get to God. Relating to neighbours and strangers is the way that we can show what we believe and how that forms our lives. So if 'blessed are the poor', and God's blessing goes to them, and if we should be trying to imitate God and show that blessing, then one major area which we must concentrate on is our poverty of community. This includes the poor and deprived of Jesus' time and ours – not because they are physically poor, but because God gives them what we fail to give them.

If we are followers of Jesus – excluding no-one, favouring through our actions the vulnerable and outcast – then we must concentrate on those our society does not, whose lives are difficult, who cannot relate, who have been the worst victims of our present society. And we have many chances to do that already in every part of our world. Youth, children, the homeless, the materially poor, but also in our culture those who have retreated into an isolated TV/mobile phone/game-led culture and who are unable to relate – they are all waiting for a community which includes them. We can then begin to bless the new poor, those who have lost the way to relate to each other as Jesus related to his followers. We are also responsible for changing things, and will not be specially blessed until we do so.

An important thinker for me is someone I met a couple of times in a theological college run on community lines in Costa Rica. Elsa Tamez[3] always makes me think of a people poor in a different way but still blessed by God. In that very male-dominated culture of Central America with a majority church which never ordains women, she taught theology in a college which refused to take a male student unless there were an equal number of women there too. Equality is just one of the things that she fights for. But most important to her as the Professor of Biblical Studies was how God speaks to the people who are around her – the poor.

For Tamez, we have first to try to understand the difficult circumstances of the first century community in the same way

---

[3] Elsa Tamez (1982) Bible of the Oppressed, Orbis

that Jesus would. Somewhat echoing Soares-Prabhu, she writes,

> *The Good News takes a very concrete form. The central message is this: the situation cannot continue as it is; impoverishment and exploitation are not God's will.* (p.67)

There are many who want to preserve their privileges or prefer not to see that following Jesus has wide social and political implications. They will say Jesus came to save us from sin – and identify that with the personal actions that society sees as wrong; drug taking, binge drinking, etc., which do lead to other wrongdoing. But because the reign of God is the reign of justice, we should not reduce the gospel of life to a simple behavioural change. For Tamez, that kind of moral teaching *'amounts to nothing but a set of patches designed to cover over the great sin that lies underneath: oppression at the national and international, the individual and collective levels. The message of the Good News is the liberation of human beings from everything and everyone that keeps them enslaved'.* (p.68)

Tamez then examines some of the great sections of Luke's Gospel that were familiar to me years ago as a choirboy. She begins with Mary, who sang to her cousin Elizabeth,

> *He has scattered the proud in the imagination of their hearts, he has put down the mighty from their thrones and exalted those of low degree; he has filled the hungry with good things, and the rich he has sent empty away.* (Luke 1:51-53, RSV)

Her song was sung at a time of celebration, and if we see that song as really representing her views, Jesus certainly had the right mother – not meek and mild, but convinced about the need for justice in society.

Jesus' first recorded sermon has that theme too, simply reading from Isaiah; saying one sentence and sitting down,

> *He has sent me to proclaim release to the captives and recovery of sight to the blind, to set at liberty those who are oppressed, to proclaim the acceptable year of the Lord.* (Luke 4:18-19, RSV)

He added: *'Today this scripture has been fulfilled in your hearing'.* (Luke 4:21, RSV)

Leonardo Bosch, another Latin American theologian and often at odds with the Vatican, has reminded us that liberation does not yet mean liberty:

> *Today there are people who believe that simply because they know the church's dogmas and the books of the Bible, or because they receive communion, they have a share in the kingdom of God. But they are wrong. Jesus himself said 'Not everyone who says to me, 'Lord, Lord,' shall enter the kingdom of heaven, but he who does the will of my father who is in heaven* (Matthew 7:21, RSV)

Issues in Christian Life

The most useful series of lectures I attended in my years of theological study was from a person whose roots were in Judaism. He dealt with the Old Testament in the order it was written, which exposed the development of a mature understanding of God. Samson and Delilah was probably the earliest story, and the first five books (including the creation stories) were written much later. One clue we were given for that timescale was the camel, which the writer of Genesis had assumed was around at the time of the patriarchs but was apparently not domesticated until much later. Human understanding of God developed over the years, and was influenced by historical events and the prevailing culture.[4] This development has continued ever since; what was once right might now be wrong, which means we can look at the aim or purpose of an ancient text rather than its detail.

Acceptance of every part of scripture as God's will as well as his Word seems impossible to justify. This was underlined in a BBC Radio 4 Thought for the Day by John Bell, who commented on the Song of Songs:

> *It's attributed to King Solomon, who certainly knew quite a bit about the subject* [healthy erotic sex] *having 700 wives and 300 concubines. Curiously he – though a direct ancestor of Jesus – is never taken as a model of good practice. Nor is Isaac: he's the son of Abraham, who is one of a number of biblical patriarchs with unusual dating practices. It's his father, who sends a servant to find a wife for the boy. Subsequently, the servant brings back home a girl called Rebecca to meet a man whom she has never seen, and who no sooner meets her than he takes her into his tent and beds her in consolation for the death of his mother.* [5]

---

[4] The way this affects current issues is explored in 'Homophobia', available as a download from
http://www.gileadbookspublishing.com/when-you-are-dying-additional-chapters.html

[5] John Bell, Thought for the Day, BBC Radio 4, 18th July 2008

There are also parts of well-known texts which are difficult to accept: the second part of the famous psalm beginning *'By the rivers of Babylon'* (Psalm 137) ends *'O daughter of Babylon, who are to be destroyed, happy the one who repays you as you have served us! Happy the one who takes and dashes your little ones against the rock!'* (NKJV). Why rejoice in and romanticise the first part and ignore the second?

All this makes it difficult to argue, as some Christians have done, that the whole Bible is the 'infallible Word of God'. What was once believed to be good for community cohesion might today have the opposite effect. We do not accept all the harsh rules of the Old Testament about warfare, racism, cruel punishment for offences, or killing of religious opponents. We cannot condone 'ethnic cleansing' by a God who in scripture orders the driving out and killing of original inhabitants to create the 'promised land' ('After the Lord your God has destroyed the people whose land he is giving you...' Deuteronomy 19:1, GNB). If we take literally the early Old Testament version of God he would be found guilty of ethnic cleansing and convicted at The Hague. How different from Isaiah's vision of the 'Peaceful Kingdom'!

As previous chapters suggest, Jesus himself was concerned with action. That action was dictated by principles which should apply to all our lives, and not by ancient rules. Jesus changed the rules but by his actions made his Principles obvious. The world has changed enormously since that time, but his morality can still be applied to modern issues. What would Jesus make of the issues which are dividing Churches and communities today, and what are we doing about them as Churches in the UK? If we gave real support to teachers, social workers, local councillors and all who work so hard in our local communities, then we could ourselves begin to bless the new poor, those who have lost the way to relate to each other.

Below I look briefly at a few areas in which I have a personal interest, and which are currently somewhat divisive within the religious communities, expanding on how we should link Jesus' Principles to today's life issues and how Christians and their churches should react or think proactively.

'Outsiders' and Women

Understanding of God grew slowly, as did the understanding of the way people should deal with each other. The Old Testament is certainly not always negative to outside people, with the story of Hagar perhaps the most significant (Genesis 16:1-16, 21:8-21). This Egyptian slave girl is taken on by Abram to bear children. Tension between her and Sara leads her to flee once she realises she is pregnant. Significantly she is in Sinai, where laws acquired by the people of Israel included *'you shall not wrong or oppress a resident alien ... If you do abuse them, when they cry out to me, I will surely heed their cry'* (Exodus 22:21-23, NRSV). In the words of Trevor Dennis, she 'is one of just four people in Genesis to hear the language of promise from God's own lips, and she a woman, a slave, an Egyptian'.[6] A great nation will result from the birth of her son, Ishmael. Dennis sees this as one of a number of annunciations in scripture, but then goes further: 'for the appearance of Gabriel to Mary, Luke took the Hagar passage. Hagar, then, turns out to be the Mary, the Madonna of the Old Testament, or one of them at least, for Hannah will be another. In one sense, if we compare her to Mary, the honour done to

---

[6] Trevor Dennis, Sarah Laughed, SPCK, 1994, p67

Hagar is the more remarkable' (p.69). This is because it is God himself and not an angel who speaks to Hagar. And this was the abused slave, not of the chosen nationality or faith.

The most significant story of Jesus' encounter with a woman is that of the gentile, a Phoenician from Syria (Mark 7:24-30) discussed in Chapter 8. In answer to her request for her daughter to be healed, Jesus tells her *'let the children be satisfied first; it is not fair to take the children's bread and throw it to the dogs'* (NEB) – meaning Jews should get the message of salvation first. Her challenge is that the message should go wider. The food is partly wasted, it falls from the table and there are plenty of 'dogs' ready to receive it; healing is for all. Some see this as Jesus testing the woman and not really denying the chance of healing on race or religious grounds. For others it is the unique time when the human part of Jesus is challenged and he accepts that he is wrong. The one who achieves this is a gentile woman from another country.

Christians and other faiths

The good Samaritan is the hero who is often seen to demonstrate the 'principles rather than rules' aspect of Jesus' teaching, but it is not just about showing up those religious leaders who were obsessed with purity. It is also about how someone from a rival group has a better understanding of how God wants us to be.

In Luke 7:1-10 we hear of the good centurion who had built a synagogue for the local Jewish community. His servant needed healing but all Jesus was required to do was to *'say the word'* and he would be healed. Jesus says *'I tell you, nowhere, even in Israel, have I found faith like this'* (Luke 7:9, NEB).

Another encounter came from breaking the rules of two faiths. Again it is a Samaritan, but this time a woman at a well whom Jesus asks for water. They both break their rules in having a dialogue which leads to a proclamation about living water followed by the conversion of many in the woman's town of Sychar through her testimony. A Samaritan woman thus becomes the first evangelist in John's gospel (John 4:4-26; 39-42).

Church action

The Archbishop of York, John Sentamu, addressed a meeting of 'Youth for Christ' in September 2008.[7] He praised the involvement of churches and Christians in community life – 22,000 Christian charities working in England and Wales, 540 of them involved in the Make Poverty History campaign and encouraging the Millennium Development goals. 23 million hours of *voluntary* work are given each year just by members of the Church of England. Commenting on the problems around external support (many trusts and other funders are suspicious of or barred from funding faith-based groups), he said *'Of course there will be those who say the Church has no role to play in service delivery and that faith has no part to play in the solution. But the facts tell a different story.'* He then gave the figures quoted above, and continued, *'Far from fitting in to the stereotype of proselytising organisations which seek to bang each other over the head with their holy books, the report found that people of faith were involved not to score points or claim spiritual scalps, but simply to help those in need. The Church has a role to play because it is based in the community. It does not*

---

[7] John Sentamu, 11 Sep 2008, www.bishopthorpepalace.co.uk/1964

drive in to places of strife in the morning and leave before the lights go down. The Church remains as part of the community and where there is hurt, the Church shares that hurt, is part of it, and is hence uniquely placed to be part of the solution'. (This theme is taken further in the chapter 'What Now?' which notes a 2008 Church of England report on its place in every community).

What gives me confidence is that I have already experienced this. At some level it is within each of our church communities. The wonderful mixed congregation in Peckham was certainly the biggest group of people I ever had a relationship with, and the completely different group in rural Rockwell Green in Somerset has been the most welcoming and sympathetic group. In both those places, though they are very different, that example of community, a hazy glimpse of Isaiah's vision, needs to be shown to the outside world and especially to the poor. They are the group in society whom Jesus spoke of more than any other and, in our time, they are not just the materially poor, though that group has even more to cope with. While, as John Sentamu says, we should not aim at conversion, it would help us all to relate to each other if we learned to follow Jesus' Principles, whatever we or those outside the Church believe about him as a person, and even without mentioning him at all.

And less TV, a few more shared meals and a bit of talking together would help too!

CHANGING LIVES

Facing death in a totally unexpected way has brought me to wrestle with some of the life-and-death issues which confront us in Britain today; these are explored in the following two chapters.

Issues around the beginning and end of life are frequently controversial; decisions about them by governments and at the personal level can cause major divisions both within Christianity and between Christians and secular groups. Questions about the value of life and who should have the right to begin or end it are in the news all the time – from advances in stem cell research to abortion; from assisted suicide (usually at Dignitas in Switzerland, which has been attacked for some of its methodology), to the use of condoms to help prevent transmission of HIV.

Whatever may be the current hot topic for ethical debate, behind it will be humanity's endless concern about the value of life itself and, especially, how to change it for the better. This is explored in Chapter 11 on Human Embryology. That research could change the lives of those with Motor Neurone Disease and therefore has a particular interest for me. And then there is the debate about how and when we should be allowed to die – also of obvious interest to me – and explored in Chapter 10.

In looking at these issues it is important to be aware of differing Christian views on our responsibilities for life. On origin, there is little dispute – Christians generally agree that God is responsible – but on humanity's resulting responsibility there are big differences in understanding how we should deal with major life issues.

Whether they are 'Creationist' or not, many believe that we should leave it all to God – aside from controlling pain, pastoral care and actions which do not interfere with God's intention for our lives. Fundamental decisions about life can never be made by the created. Abortion can never be allowed; people must die naturally and embryology can never involve human cells. This is backed up with passages from scripture such as James 2.26 *'the body without the spirit is dead'* (GNB). Fundamentally the soul brings life and, just as at the beginning of all human life, we must respect God's role in deciding when life should begin or end.

Other Christians interpret the creation story very differently. Rather than being given no power over life, God gives Adam dominion over everything on earth (Genesis 2: 18). Richard Harries spoke on how we must develop the responsibility given to us:

> *... for us human beings it would be unnatural just to let nature take its course. That is what happens with the birds and the bees, but we are different. We have rational minds, and wills to choose. What is natural for us is that we use the minds God has given us to interact with natural processes in order to enhance human well-being.* [1]

He was speaking about human embryology but his words could apply more widely.

None of these issues are easy to deal with, and many of us hold ambivalent or contradictory views. We may be strongly opposed to 'social abortion' (sometimes practiced in societies

---

[1] Rt. Rev Lord Richard Harries, BBC Thought for the Day, 31 October 2008.

where male children are preferred to female) but we might think differently about victims of rape, women who might die in childbirth, or children who will be born deformed. Prevention is also a divisive issue – do you give 'pregnancy prevention assistance' to under 16s? Some Christians object to both contraception and abortion as they curtail potential life. But the former might prevent the latter. Most people would prefer abortion not to happen at all but many accept that it must happen sometimes.

These dilemmas are discussed among theologians and senior figures in our faiths, such as at a 2008 meeting in Rome between the Pope and Muslim leaders. Abdal Hakim Murad, the Muslim chaplain at Cambridge University, spoke of the challenge individual cases present and cited an example which occurred immediately after that meeting,

> *In his lecture, the Pope praised Muslim commitment to serving the needy, and issued a clarion call for a deeper co-operation between Christians and Muslims, who share a belief in the sanctity of life.* [2]

Murad then came home to news about Hannah Jones, the thirteen-year-old who had won her battle with a hospital to refuse treatment and be allowed to die at home. He continued,

> *My dilemma was this. In Rome we had certainly agreed to care about the suffering sick, irrespective of their religion. But our brave talk about human dignity was couched in rather simple, cut-and-dried phrases about the sanctity of human life. Confronted with the Hannah Jones case, it*

---

[2] Abdal Hakim Murad, BBC, Thought for the Day, 14 November 2008

didn't seem to offer an unambiguous answer to her dilemma.

He reminded us that Islam is clear about the sanctity of life but patience in adversity is also seen to be 'noble'. He quoted the Qur'an, which suggests giving 'good news' to those who 'patiently endure' and know they will return to God. He summarised,

> *Life is God's gift and we must strive, and if necessary suffer, to preserve it. But is there always dignity in a life where medical science postpones death at the cost of a thousand side-effects? Do we believe in a God who wants us to linger, come what may?*

Murad has identified a key problem faced by individuals, faith groups and law makers. For faith groups, the understanding of God's will is crucial. Any complexities are generally dismissed by those Christians who believe we have been given divine rules which cannot be changed. However, many of them would be supporters of the death penalty, which is a human decision. As with issues such as the role of women in ministry and homosexuality, their views are based on selective use of scripture.

Solutions are much more difficult for Christians like me who uphold both the interpretation of scripture and modern medical science. We have to balance deeply-held beliefs with the understanding that all people have been given the freedom and ability through our consciences to make right decisions.

These opposing views are based primarily on different interpretations of the Creation stories – the role we humans have been given by God. I believe that, as with everything else, these issues can only be settled by applying the Principles of Jesus to the responsibility given to us.

CHAPTER 10

Assisted Suicide

In January 2003 Reginald Crew, suffering, like me, from Motor Neurone Disease, became the first British person known to have travelled to Dignitas in Switzerland for assistance in dying. He would have preferred it to have happened at home. While the number of people travelling from the UK to Dignitas has grown, numbers are still low, partly because of cost and physical difficulties. Another limiting factor is that any assisting friends or relatives might have legal action taken against them here. Though no such person has yet been convicted, all attempts so far to turn this lack of action into a legal exemption from prosecution have failed.

Daniel James was a more recent case of assisted suicide; a young man, injured and partially paralysed, he was certain he would never again be able to play rugby and therefore felt life was not worth living. Many, including Matt Hampson, to whom much the same had happened from a similar rugby accident, felt that if he had waited longer he might have thought differently. New examples seem to be in the news all the time. In July 2009 we heard of an unusual case; the conductor Sir Edward Downes, in his mid-eighties and ill but not terminally, joined his younger wife Joan, who had cancer, and supported by their children, they died together at Dignitas.

The slightly different issue of permitted death, though also centring on who should make the decision, came to public attention towards the end of 2008 when Debbie Purdy challenged the UK legal system to allow it. She is suffering from multiple sclerosis and, while not yet at the stage when she is contemplating it, believes that permitted death should be possible here in Britain. The Law Lords, in their last decision, agreed that clarification is needed so that people would know when assistance was permitted. In a radio interview Debbie Purdy pointed out that the original law had been passed in 1961 when palliative care was patchy and treatment for cancer in particular was very poor.

In the news around the same time was thirteen-year-old Hannah, whose hospital wanted her to have a heart replacement. She was in a weak condition partly because of drugs given since her diagnosis when she was very young. As the success of the proposed operation was uncertain, she wanted instead to die at home. The hospital took her to court, claiming that she did not have the right to decide. Later, they withdrew the case.

The Royal College of Nurses became the first medical group to adopt a neutral attitude to this issue when, in July 2009, 49 per cent of a survey approved the right to assisted suicide and only 40 per cent objected to it.

Choosing to die

'Suicidal' behaviour in the service of others is much honoured, especially in its military context. Many posthumous awards of the Victoria Cross are for those who, deliberately or not, have given their lives for others. Similarly, there is the tradition of 'women and children first', and stories of parents who save their children from a burning house only to perish themselves as the blaze worsens. In the civilian world, Captain Lawrence Oates is the man who comes immediately to my mind. Suffering from severe frostbite, he left Captain Robert Scott and others in their Antarctic tent, with his famous farewell words *'I am just going outside and may be some time'*.

Risk-taking has been the choice of many Christians. As part of my theological training I had a year at St. Augustine's College in Canterbury. Formerly used for missionary training, one wall of the chapel crypt had scores of bricks on which the departure date and death of missionaries were recorded – sometimes within a few months of each other. In West Africa in particular, those following God's call would know their very survival was doubtful. It was as if God was testing them, or at least asking them to be prepared to die. Suicides have differing causes, often the result of mental health problems, frequently linked to the deterioration or ending of relationships – people jumping off bridges or cliffs, or asphyxiation from car exhaust fumes. Being prepared to die, whether for one's own reasons or for other people, is an enormous decision; while other people may be part of the reason, the choice to die is made personally. But 'assisted death' is very different. It is not someone assisting his friend by driving him to a nearby cliff. It requires forethought and professional skill, as proposed by the campaign group Dignity in Dying:

> *An assisted death is where a doctor prescribes a life-ending dose of medication to a mentally competent, terminally ill adult at their request and subject to safeguards, and the patient then chooses to administer the medication themselves.* [1]

It is claimed that four-fifths of British adults support the idea of assisted death, but government, churches and many other

---

[1] www.dignityindying.org.uk

organisations disagree. Only Belgium, Holland, Switzerland and the State of Oregon in the USA have agreed such a policy. The principal question of who is responsible for decisions about life is particularly important to religious groups, and will be dealt with later; but it is also central to each of the six issues explored below.

Before those six are looked at, one clarification is needed to understand the difference between assisted suicide and a 'Living Will'. The Living Will allows someone with a serious illness, such as Motor Neurone Disease, to state beforehand that they would not want to be resuscitated should another life-threatening condition develop. It generally cuts out any question of life-support machines, and limits treatment to pain relief. It is legally binding and approved by bodies as varied as the British Medical Association and Age Concern. I have one and my GP has a copy of it. It ensures that my wishes are followed when I no longer have any ability to make them known, and is very different from going to my GP and saying, *'Please give me something to kill me'.*

The Six Issues

1. Temporary or permanent change?

People have different levels of coping with suffering and differing views about whether their life is worth living. But also, as I know from personal experience, things can change from day to day. Some months ago I had a bad weekend, with sickness, high temperature and severe whole-body juddering. I felt this might be the beginning of the end. If so, I wanted to die then. Shame I wouldn't finish things I wanted to do, but at least I had written farewell letters to my wife and children. I hoped my 'Living Will' would become operative and that I would not be resuscitated in any way, as I was already dying. But will the time come when I want someone to help me to die? Would I even have the courage?

That account is there not to provoke sympathy but to emphasise the way things change even during the course of general decline. My Motor Neurone Disease is progressive rather than sudden and there have certainly been times, more than just the one mentioned above, when death was something I was both expecting very soon and hoping would come. This is not true at the moment, though I am physically much weaker than before.

A variation in personal feelings can also come through the effect of certain drugs. I have painkillers four times a day through my 'PEG' directly into my stomach, and I have also had 'patches' for the same purpose. What we noticed was that when any of these drugs included opiates, I tended to feel more negative about my future. Though I would not say I was 'depressed', combined with other things, specific drugs could influence my attitude.

I have also felt 'down' rather than 'up' when some new devices have arrived. One was early on – a seat came to go over the bath so I could sit and have a shower. It worked for a while but meant I would never again lie soaking in a bath. However, I came to accept it and now quite enjoy my showers on the commode. Later I was able to have some real baths at the local hospice. At many stages during my decline I have thought, 'If it stops here, I could live with it'.

These are all examples of the kind of things that are used in the secular argument against assisted suicide – there are solutions to many problems, drug treatment can be modified and time can change a person's view of events.

2. Palliative care

Both sides of the assisted-suicide argument agree that improved palliative care would benefit nearly everyone; some see it as almost all that is needed but others as merely delaying the inevitable and failing to tackle the real issue of choice. Some, such as the Motor Neurone Disease Association, have not taken sides but campaign for palliative care:

> The MND Association neither supports nor opposes any attempt to change the law regarding euthanasia or assisted suicide because we believe it is a matter of individual conscience and it is not for the Association to make judgements. However, in advance of any change in the law, we are campaigning to ensure that the very best palliative and terminal care is available to everyone who needs it. Only then will anyone considering ending his or her life early genuinely have a choice. [2]

A House of Lords Select Committee found that better palliative care would not change the minds of those whose suffering derives from learning that they have a terminal illness rather than from any symptoms; they are more likely to support assisted suicide. The Committee also heard from a consultant in palliative care that the same applied to people with strong personalities who wish to be in control of every aspect of their lives; they find it difficult to deal with what is happening now, or think of what the future might bring. [3]

---

[2] www.mndassociation.org
[3] Select Committee Report HL 86-I, p. 83

While the cost of care is an issue in many countries, the Church of England claims that the quality of palliative care and financial support in the UK is among the best in the world and therefore no change in the law is needed. Their response to the House of Lords bill included this as part of their conclusion:

> *The Bill is unnecessary. When death is imminent or inevitable there is at present no legal or moral obligation to give medical treatment that is futile or burdensome. It is both moral and legal now for necessary pain relief to be given, even if it is likely that death will be hastened as a result. But that is not murder or assisted suicide. What terminally ill people need is to be cared for, not to be killed. They need excellent palliative care including proper and effective regimes for pain relief. They need to be treated with the compassion and respect that this bill would put gravely at risk.* [4]

That response understands the shift from acute to palliative care, acknowledging that the patient needs to be allowed to die. Giving pain-relieving drugs which are known to accelerate death is not seen as intentional killing, if the aim is to relieve acute pain. Experienced medical staff, carers and probably relatives will all consult, but the patient might not be able to take a part in decisions. That is when it can be useful to have signed a Living Will. An opposing view is that failing to give life-prolonging drugs, or giving any which are known to shorten life, with the possibility of patient non-involvement, is as morally debatable as assisted suicide.

---

[4] www.cofe.anglican.org/info/euthanasia

Dignity in Dying, while supporting improved palliative care, does not believe it is adequate in every case. In its 'Vision for End-of-Life Care', this is one of seven proposals:

> *There would be a sensible acknowledgement from health care professionals and decision-makers that palliative care cannot meet the needs of all dying patients. No amount of good palliative care can address some patient's concerns regarding their loss of autonomy, loss of dignity and loss of control. Therefore, patient choice should include the right of terminally ill adults, within strict safeguards, to have the option of an assisted death.* [5]

Standards of palliative care are important, but to see this as something which solves all dilemmas ignores some non-medical questions – on which opinions are also divided.

3. Dignity

In a Thought for the Day on BBC Radio 4, Catherine Pepinster detailed the importance of the word 'dignity':

> *This morning we heard that doctors who argued that Baby OT should not have to endure more invasive treatment have won their court battle to – as they say – allow him to die with dignity. It's noticeable that the underlying theme of so much of the debate about dying is dignity. So powerful is the word that one organisation most connected with euthanasia is called Dignity in Dying*

---

[5] www.dignityindying.org.uk

while the Zurich clinic where some Britons have gone to commit assisted suicide is called Dignitas. [6]

She described dignity as *'about being someone'* and then said *'what dignity really means – to be honoured'*.

Is dignity personal or universal? One argument is that any weakening of the principle of saving life at any cost will undermine the dignity of the whole of humanity and encourage those wanting further relaxation. (These questions are dealt with below in 'Slippery Slope', and in the paragraphs on Christian views).

Personal dignity, and for certain individuals particularly indignity, is much more specific. Most stories that come to our attention concern people in long-term care and are often about being left for hours with parts of the body exposed in a public area of the care home or being neglected when there is a known problem of incontinence. While this is not directly related to assisted suicide, quality of care and the attitude of both professionals and families are crucial. (Sadly some carers could also tell stories of physical and verbal abuse by patients.)

Dignity means different things to different people, and we can sometimes surprise ourselves by what we are able to cope with and what we find difficult. Before I was ill I would not have thought I could ever cope in public places – streets, shops, concerts, churches – with being slumped in a wheelchair, dribbling on a brightly coloured towel acting as a bib. But what demeans me are people who assume I am daft and deaf as well as unable to speak. People at church and other friends are very different because they physically come down to my wheelchair level and talk about things which they know

---

[6] Catherine Pepinster, Thought for the Day, 21 March 2009

interest me such as birds and music but, above all, their vocabulary and volume are both normal. A second annoyance is being ignored, especially when I know the answer to a problem or, if I am in pain, finding that other things are given priority. (Sadly, the worst example was in a hospice, where I was on an apparent 'dummy run', with staff trying to find the right way to use the equipment to get me from bed to bath. I was lying on a hard surface in greater pain than I had experienced for many months but, since I could not speak, was being ignored while they discussed what to do next.)

To whom should priority be given? To the individual or to those who claim to speak on behalf of 'society'? If I get to the point where I continue to be mentally active (of 'sound mind') and not clinically depressed, yet feel that life has no purpose because I am no longer capable of operating in any way, or that my dignity has become so eroded that I resent my life being dominated by care routines, should I not be helped to die? Or do I have to wait for pneumonia or another painful secondary disease before I could be allowed to die? It is as if the only real pain is physical and it has to be gone through to earn enough points.

Dignity is important for everyone, but difficult to legislate for as it needs to balance the concerns of the individual, the family and the doctor. For the individual, the issue is obviously personal and resolvable by a change in attitude from those close to them, family and carers in particular. This is neither simple nor easy, but would make the physical and emotional pain more bearable. It would mean changes in priorities, especially in care homes which put a lot of pressure on staff to complete their rotas of everyday tasks.

4. Families

There are at least two major motivations affecting the families of severely ill people. Many are concerned to help end the suffering of someone close to them. Sadly some others may be tempted to put pressure on the one who is seriously ill because they can see a financial or other advantage if the sick person were to choose to die.

In any one case, family and friends may have very different views from each other, and this could be because of religious or other convictions, understanding of the disease, or recent contact with and closeness to the dying. Friends or family will clearly be affected and a request for assisted suicide places demands on those who have to accept a decision they might not agree with. There might also be guilt at not being involved enough, unresolved family issues, basic ignorance or perhaps unwillingness to accept the reality.

My main concern is for Gaby's life. She copes with all of the domestic duties which we used to share and, apart from a maximum of nine hours of carers per week, she looks after me the whole time. She has acknowledged that I am already not the person she wants to remember. I cannot speak, help in the garden, eat or make anything in the kitchen. I cannot join her walking in the glorious Quantock Hills or, in reality, do anything without her help. The 'me' she knew has gone. This does not mean I feel less loved – the opposite is true – but we have both changed and we are the only ones who really understand the situation. We should be able to decide if and when an end could or should be planned.

Writing 'Arguments for and against' for the BBC website, Dr. Trisha Macnair asks, 'How can we be sure that a person really wants to die and isn't being taken advantage of, for financial reasons, for example?' [7] In the following section on 'Voluntary Euthanasia' this is also the main theme:

> *Voluntary euthanasia simply emphasises that the choice to die has been made voluntarily by the person in question, rather than imposed on them by legal or social rules. However, opponents of euthanasia often argue that it can be very difficult to be sure that someone's request is truly voluntarily made. For example, an elderly person requiring expensive healthcare may feel that they're such a burden to relatives that they should request euthanasia. There's also the risk that people being treated with powerful painkillers or cancer drugs may not be in a sufficiently clear state of mind or competent enough to make an informed and balanced judgement.*

As would be expected, Dignity in Dying have a different view. For them, once it is legal, people will have access to proper counseling, there will be an End-of-Life Care Plan, and their GP and social workers will know of their case. They see this as much more secure than the current solution where assisted suicide is only available by travelling outside the UK.

I do understand the pressure which some terminally ill people may feel. Comments such as 'This all takes so long,' or 'My back hurts so much when I do this,' might seem innocuous, but their effect depends on tone, frequency and context and, above all, on the depth of the relationship; do both carer and cared-for understand that both lives have changed, individually and collectively?

---

[7] www.bbc.co.uk/health/support/terminalillness_euthanasia.shtml #arguments_for_and_against

5. Doctors

In 1994 a House of Lords Select Committee reported on a visit to the Netherlands (the current law there, passed in 2002, does not allow assisted suicide but does not prosecute doctors who report what they have done). During this visit they found that some doctors were not following the rules. They were *'concerned that vulnerable people – the elderly, lonely, sick or distressed – would feel pressure, whether real or imagined, to request early death...the message which society sends to vulnerable and disadvantaged people should not, however obliquely, encourage them to seek death, but should assure them of our care and support.'* [8]

While this is worrying, it does not automatically apply to the UK, any more than suggesting that our trusted GP might be anything like the mass murderer, Dr. Shipman. More important to most people is the shift in principles – doctors are there to care and cure, not to assist and certainly not to suggest a patient's death. But if someone in pain wishes to die, why cannot they have the right to ask the medical professional who knows them best to help them?

But is every doctor sufficiently skilled in difficult areas such as long-term suffering or psychological pressures? For some people who wish to keep the status quo, even aspects of palliative care – in which painkillers can be given with the known side-effect of hastening death – can look like a step towards giving permission to omit crucial stages of treatment. And would doctors be the best people to deal with family matters – finance and the other issues mentioned above? This

---

[8] HL 86-I, paragraphs 238-9

is hugely variable and will become increasingly difficult as families disperse.

I think a strict code of conduct could cope with all the identified problems, but opposition by some doctors would mean piecemeal availability, probably mainly in the private sector.

6. Slippery Slope

This sixth issue is very closely linked to the previous one. Once doctors are allowed the possibility of helping people to die, one argument is that it will become just a part of the scenario for every patient. Some add in the cost element, to the individual and to the family as well as publicly-funded health care costs. Terminally ill patients have high hospital bed occupation, drug and personnel costs, so if the patient is dying anyway, should they not be made aware of all the options?

The worst scenario expands this to include the increasing number of vulnerable old people whose illnesses might be serious, painful and long-lasting, but are not terminal. Are the needs of a relatively small number of individuals more important than the common good? Even if the policy is well thought through and each case is approved by both specialist doctors and counsellors, what seems right for one individual makes others more vulnerable. If life tacitly becomes less valuable, would the next campaign be less liberal – the return of the death penalty? The counter argument, as always, is that once it is legal there would be wider public knowledge and strict regulations which would prevent abuse.

Logic or simply belief?

Many who argue from one side or the other are coming from positions which dictate the views they will take. Someone devoted to individual human rights would support the principle that assisted suicide is a right, and therefore claim that doctors would behave professionally, and the legal code would ensure that no-one was abused. They might even quote Albert Schweitzer,

> *We must all die. But that I can save (a person) from days of torture, that is what I feel as my great and ever new privilege. Pain is a more terrible lord of mankind than even death himself.* [9]

On the other side, many would raise concerns about the change in the role of doctors and they would certainly advocate good palliative care as the solution to many problems. The churches are the biggest group opposed to any changes but, as shown below, tend to use spiritual arguments when dealing with legislation. Medical knowledge and prosperity have increased so much, in the developed world at least, that old examples and rules do not always apply. Official church statements for internal use focus on life being in God's hands and not ours rather than on selected Bible verses. Self-sacrifice and the possibility of martyrdom have long been accepted Christian virtues but in God's name, not the modern phenomenon of suicide bombing by a terrorist fanatic.

---

[9] Albert Schweitzer (1953) On the Edge of the Primeval Forest, London: Adam and Charles Black

Suicide in the Bible

Jesus does not mention suicide (any more than he does homosexuality), though some people argue that he willed his own death – a misunderstanding of his inevitable persecution by the authorities. But it is worth looking at earlier biblical examples and how they were seen.

Suicide is there in the Bible, certainly not prominent, but neither is it seen as sinful. In the Old Testament, seeking death is often portrayed as honourable but God refuses to take part. Moses asks God to kill him because his given task is beyond him. Blaming God for the mess, he proclaims *'If you treat me like this, please kill me here and now'* (Numbers 11:15, NKJV). It is the same for Jonah: he is angry when God decides not to destroy the city of Nineveh. *'It is better to die than live,'* (Jonah 4:3, NRSV). Elijah also asks to die to escape the threatened revenge following his killing of four hundred priests of Baal (1Kings 18:40 and 19:4). God does not approve.

When God is not asked, things are different, in particular for military leaders. In Judges 9:52-54 Abimelech is about to perform genocide within Thebez when a woman hurls a lump of stone from the city walls. Injured, and believing he will die, he is so appalled that people would hear he had been killed by a woman that he asks his aide to kill him with his sword. A better-known story six chapters later has Samson pulling a building down on himself as well as many others (Judges 16:29-30). The suicide of Saul has several versions. In one, he asks his aide to kill him; he refuses and Saul falls on his own sword. The aide follows suit (1 Samuel 31:4-6). This is justified in 1 Chronicles 10:3-7 by claiming the victors would torture and abuse him. But a later report to King David in 2 Samuel 1:1-17 has Saul's suicide assisted by a stranger. There is no criticism of Saul for asking, but the assisting stranger is executed. When his city of Tizrah was successfully besieged, King Zimri saw this as a result of his sin and he stood inside his own palace, set fire to it and died (1Kings 16:15-20). Ahthophet wanted 12,000 men to attack King David. When refused, he hanged himself (2 Samuel 17:1-29).

While the odd military encounter produced what might be called 'honourable sacrifice' as people were led to defeat, there is no blanket approval of suicide and no willingness from God to be part of it.

The Matthew version of Judas' death (Matthew 27:5) certainly has this as suicide, but there is little more in the New Testament. Paul does contemplate it at one point, but it has more to do with getting to heaven faster, and he decides to continue living in this world. Revelation 9:1-10 suggests suicide will not be possible in Hell – no-one can escape eternal punishment. The issue is identified by some in 1 Corinthians 3:17, where God will destroy those who destroy the Temple. There are disagreements on the precise meaning but, while the result might be self-inflicted, this is punishment not suicide. [10]

From that limited biblical evidence it is very difficult to form any judgement except that, when asked, God does not approve of suicide. The idea of honourable death later became part of the Christian story for martyrs who, following the example of Jesus, refused to denounce their faith. Such examples are mostly acceptable to Christians and, they would believe, to God; but they do not help us with the question of assisted suicide. There are those Old Testament military examples, but

---

[10] More on the texts used here can be found at
www.religioustolerance.org

even one of those is dubious, and no-one quotes them to justify any form of suicide.

The sanctity of human life

The principle of the sanctity of life is crucial to Christians though with no specific biblical backing. It encapsulates the belief that life is itself sacred because it is given by God. Life has an inherent value, not just a conditional one. The principle is enshrined in law in the form of an absolute prohibition of the intentional killing of innocent human beings. It is not normally taken to mean that any life ought to be preserved at all costs, but it does protect all and ensure that all are equal. For a Christian, this principle also encapsulates the simple belief that my life belongs to God, not to me, and I therefore have no right to end it. Some critics dislike the word 'sanctity' because it suggests a religious prohibition that is inappropriate in a secular society.

The Church of England has produced two important statements on the issue of euthanasia. The second was prepared jointly with the Roman Catholic Church for the 2004 House of Lords debate (and is reproduced in full in Appendix B). A few years earlier, at the 1998 Lambeth Conference, this resolution was passed:

In the light of current debate and proposals for the legalisation of euthanasia in several countries, this Conference,

(a) *affirms that life is God-given and has intrinsic sanctity, significance and worth;*
(b) *defines euthanasia as the act by which one person intentionally causes or assists in causing the death of*

another who is terminally or seriously ill in order to end the other's pain and suffering;

(c)   *resolves that euthanasia, as precisely defined, is neither compatible with the Christian faith nor should be permitted in civil legislation;*

(d)   *distinguishes between euthanasia and withholding, withdrawing, declining or terminating excessive medical treatment and intervention, all of which may be consonant with Christian faith in enabling a person to die with dignity. When a person is in a permanent vegetative state, to sustain him or her with artificial nutrition and hydration may be seen as constituting medical intervention; and*

(e)   *commends the Section Report on euthanasia as a suitable introduction for study of such matters in all Provinces of the Communion.*[11]

The 2004 Report concentrates in its conclusion on the 'slippery slope', stating that euthanasia is misguided and unnecessary:

To take this step would fundamentally undermine the basis of law and medicine and undermine the duty of the state to care for vulnerable people.... The right to die would become the duty to die. [12]

---

[11] Church of England report Assisted Suicide and Voluntary Euthanasia: A Briefing Paper from the Mission and Public Affairs Council (2004) Appendix III

[12] Op. cit. Main Report, para 22.

In June 2009, it was reported that around 800 British people had registered with the Swiss agency Dignitas. More than thirty were said to be planning to go there soon. The House of Lords was about to discuss a bill, this time promoted by Lord Faulkner. Bishop Tom Butler, who had been responsible for chairing the group which produced the 2004 Church of England report, gave a 'Thought for the Day' which summarised their position. He emphasised the value and experience of hospices all over the country. He was concerned about the financial pressure which vulnerable people can feel in respect of their close family; stressing the rights of individuals could have unintended consequences: the slippery slope. He ended with a summary of the Church's position:

> *But of course, for bishops this is not primarily a legal question or even one of balance of care and protection; our position is a theological one for it grows out of our belief that God has given to humankind the gift of life and it is to be revered, cherished and preserved. It follows that all human beings are to be valued, irrespective of their condition or potential for achievement. Adherence to this principle, we believe, provides a fundamental test as to what constitutes a civilized society. Move from this and the right to die risks becoming the duty to die.* [13]

So what is important for me?

Despite the shock that I and the majority of British people felt at the misuse of MPs' expenses in 2009, I still trust them for

---

[13] Rt. Rev. Tom Butler, Thought for the Day, 9 June 2009.

non-political moral judgements about life. Historically, these areas have included capital punishment, abortion and latterly civil partnerships for gay people. More recently there was human embryology (see Chapter 11) but in 2004 and 2006 the House of Lords rejected bills on assisted suicide. Further discussion on exemption from prosecution of anyone who 'assists' has been rather strange since no-one has yet been prosecuted and what they have helped to do is itself no longer a crime.

I feel this is somewhat illogical, though it is defended by some as protecting vulnerable individuals from abuse. This is one of the main arguments against change – that the vulnerable would be put under greater pressure, especially as detailed above in 'Family'. Any proposed protection procedure might not be trusted, partly because of the scandal of repeated failures of the system to protect children. Scandal and failure draw public attention but ignore thousands of successful cases and huge numbers of dedicated staff. Mistakes are bound to be made, but in each case of assisted suicide there will be far fewer agencies and individuals involved than there are in child protection. It should be possible to devise a system which will deal with expressed anxieties. As I have already suggested, views on many of the disputed issues grow from deeply-held values. Someone arguing from a human-rights perspective would almost certainly agree with me that a protective system would work.

Most Christians will disagree, believing that God will choose the appropriate moment for all of us. This is the basis but, to be relevant to secular organisations and, in particular, to members of the House of Lords, the Churches understandably emphasise issues which are not specifically religious. Differing interpretations of the Creation stories remain fundamental. I cannot believe in a God who retains all power and allows the terrible pain and short life-span of so many people in developing countries. And has he decided I will catch pneumonia this Thursday or next? The point of the Creation stories is to teach that we are responsible for the whole world – hence the mess we are in. We can and do make mistakes but, as far as the things we can control are concerned, we are responsible.

Strangely, a sermon I heard recently on Ascension Sunday took the same theme. Just as a parent teaching a child to ride a bike will let go of the saddle in the knowledge that this will lead to more confidence and competence as well as more responsibility, so Jesus directed and guided us and then left us so we could fulfil our potential. On both secular and sacred grounds – at least for Christians – we have a duty to care for life. While the priority must always be protection of the world's poor, those who suffer in a personal way have both the right and responsibility to decide their own future, considering family and other relationships.

Assisted suicide should therefore be allowed – though two recent happenings have underlined for me the need for professional guidance. The first was receiving a quotation sent by a psychotherapist friend. It gave a new perspective to the idea of compassion:

> *Some suggest that compassion reveals more about our difficulty in seeing others in pain than the actual pain that others experience. Thus action to remove pain altogether, for example by euthanasia, would be really to relieve ourselves rather than the sufferer. Of course, feelings of compassion are often genuine, but mere feeling is not sufficient to make a difference to the patient. Thus for any*

action taken on the basis of compassion, we need to ensure, as far as possible, that it will help the situation. [14]

The other piece of input was anonymous. Coming out of church that same Ascension Sunday, we found an envelope under the wiper blade of our wheelchair-friendly van. Inside was a leaflet; 'Join Dignity in Dying'. Was someone upset at seeing this dribbling, slumped, uncommunicative wheelchair-user or were they very supportive of the principles and simply giving information? My reaction was more emotional than I expected. Someone with whom I even shared the 'Peace' wanted me to die! Later, I was perhaps more logical – was it from someone who faces the same decision as me? But why the anonymity? To avoid upsetting relatives was the only reason I could think of. Whatever the real reason behind the action and my reaction, I certainly had a surprisingly odd feeling of pressure, although this was nowhere near the level of potential family pressure suggested by those opposed to any changes in the law.

For me, while I am very aware of my emotions (perhaps due to particular medication) I remain convinced that we need a system which does not just start when physical pain or other kinds of suffering become unbearable.

Most churches seem to agree that assisted suicide is wrong but I disagree with their position. Like the majority of people, I hope to die peacefully one night. However, if deterioration continues as predicted, when communication becomes even more difficult or I need a constant supply of oxygen, then most of the value life still has for me will have gone. I am already not

[14] David Cook (1983) The Moral Maze: A Way of Exploring Christian Ethics, pp. 158-9.

the 'real me'. Would I have the courage to ask for my life to be ended? At present, I doubt it, but maybe that bit of me will change too.

Chapter 11

Human Embryology

One of the projects I used to recruit for a few years ago was Shisong Hospital in the north-west region of Cameroon. It was run by Roman Catholic Franciscan sisters who also had a nurse training school, a centre to treat and train disabled people, an orphanage, clinics in even more remote areas, and many community projects. While founded by Italian sisters, they needed English-speaking staff and volunteers.

The sisters were a lively group of women who, despite having to live under the rules of their order, probably had more independence and security than many in the local community. They were therefore very careful about adding to their 300 or so members, but had accepted as a novice one of the volunteers we had sent to help in their administration – much to the annoyance of her parents, who might never see her again.

The sisters were in two disputes with the Cameroon government. One was about money; they still had links with Italy and especially with a hospital in Milan, which had taken Cameroon staff for training and some young patients with cardiac problems. They were now at the next stage – the setting up of the Cameroon's first specialist cardiac unit for children. The Cameroon government wanted to put the unit in a state hospital but the Milan hospital knew of Cameroon's very poor standing in the world corruption table and wanted their support not to disappear into already well-filled pockets.

The second disagreement was around the CAF, the initials for both the Cameroon currency (Central African Franc) and their

HIV/AIDS campaign (Condoms, Abstinence and Faithfulness). The sisters, along with the rest of their church, scratched out the 'C' (sometimes literally), and were therefore accused by some officials of encouraging AIDS. It was a difficult decision. The Roman Catholic rule on condoms was made long before AIDS was an issue, and is about 'killing the seeds of life'. It is difficult for many to accept that this dogma could be more important than stopping the spread of a life-threatening disease. It is obviously better if abstinence and faithfulness are adhered to, but they are not. In the English Roman Catholic Church birth control is seen to be a matter of conscience, though still officially sinful; there is an understanding that smaller families, better personal relationships and decreased infection can result.

The big issues of life are complex, and compromise is sometimes necessary – for example in the question of abortion where the life of the mother might otherwise be at risk. Human embryology is a current example of such a dilemma; it divides both churches and politicians and, for many people, ties the preservation of some lives in the future to the creation and ending of life. It takes us far deeper into life issues than simply removing the 'C'.

A good decision

The British Parliament voted in favour of the proposal to allow a new form of research which would implant human material into an animal cell for up to fourteen days. It seems the issue itself is settled, though other parts of the bill concerning abortion created delay to the next parliamentary reading. The debate, however, revealed some big issues that divide Christians on whether it is right to re-interpret scripture and ancient doctrines that were laid down long before modern science offered unthought-of possibilities. I have chosen to investigate the issue partly because it cuts deeply into those differences of opinion over our responsibilities for life.

In looking at the human embryology issue I have also to admit a large element of self-interest. Researchers into the still-unknown cause of Motor Neurone Disease are seeing the proposed procedures as one possibility of eventual easier diagnosis and cure. It will not help me, but might help future sufferers.

Not every MND patient would agree. Michael Wenham is a parish priest also suffering from the disease but with much slower degeneration than mine.[1] In a newspaper article he said,

> *Personally, it seems to me to be downright perverse to create human life (however embryonic) only to destroy it a fortnight later. In fact I think it's immoral.* [2]

He went on to suggest alternative research methods:

> *There are sources of stem cells which do not have that moral ambiguity, such as induced pluripotent stem cells (taken from the skin) and umbilical-cord blood.*

There are therefore two linked issues to look at – the ethics of the use of human embryonic cells and the usefulness of any alternative. Faith groups tend, like Michael Wenham, to concentrate on the first, using theological argument to define the ethics and then joining secular opponents in suggesting

---

[1] Michael Wenham (2008) My Donkey Body, Monarch
[2] Church Times, 17 October 2008, pp. 20-21

alternatives. But not all Christians agree with the theological argument.

In 2009 at Easter-time the Roman Catholic Primate in Scotland, Cardinal Keith O'Brien, described a part of a government Human Fertilisation and Embryology Bill as '*grotesque*' and '*hideous*', of '*Frankenstein proportions*' and '*a monstrous attack on human rights, human dignity and human life*'.[3] The media was full of reports of how many Cabinet members or Roman Catholic MPs would vote against it. Eventually a free vote was allowed on that specific issue. Soon after, former Prime Minister Tony Blair spoke of how he felt faith communities should be involved in political decisions, even though he had down-played his personal faith while in office.

So are they both right, and is this issue one which we could look at to check that out? If church bodies ought to use their power and influence in the way I have advocated in previous chapters, should I not support Tony Blair's position? In theory, yes, but only if the New Testament, interpreted in the light of modern science, supports what is being advocated (this was explored in more detail in other chapters, especially in 7, 'Principles or Rules' and 8, 'Back to the Beginning').

Background – what is the issue?

I first had to find out what was being proposed, and begin to understand the science. For that I have to confess I started with the Motor Neurone Disease Association (MNDA) website.

Scientists need to use embryonic stem cells because they are basic cells which are not yet specialised into any specific cell

---

[3] The Daily Record, 23 March 2008

type. The hope is that research will show how to trigger these embryonic stem cells into nerve cells in the laboratory – and for MND this means investigating motor nerve cells (neurones). If successful, for the first time live human motor neurones could be used both to understand more about MND and also lead for the first time to hoped-for treatments.

The cells need to be of human origin as the research is about a specific human condition, but the shortage of human eggs (already licensed for research) has led the Human Fertilisation and Embryology Authority (HFEA) to propose the use of animal eggs, where the animal DNA has been replaced with human DNA; rabbit or cow eggs are the current possibilities. The MNDA explains the process:

> *Within mammalian cells, 99% of the DNA is stored in a compartment called the nucleus. The DNA within the nucleus of the animal egg will be removed, creating an 'egg-shell'. The next step is to insert the nucleus of a human adult cell (usually a skin cell) into this animal 'egg shell'. Human embryonic stem cells will form within this egg, as the genetic material controlling their development is 99% human.* [4]

The website then goes on to explain how in the case of MND this could only be done with donated skin cells from the 10% of sufferers who have the inherited form of the disease. It also explains the strict research guidelines and the public consultation duties of the HFEA, and adds that this is part of a much wider Act to come before Parliament.

---

[4] www.mndassociation.org/research/news_in_research/
archived_news_in_research/animal_eggs_for.html

As I understand it, from admittedly only one source, the human skin cells are allowed to grow within a separate 'egg shell' and this is because egg cells from humans are difficult to resource.

In one sense, the arguments within the Christian community over human embryology are different from those raised by issues I have looked at in other chapters (and also in articles on Peace, Christians and Other Faiths, Homosexuality and Community, which are available as downloads from www.GileadBooksPublishing.com). Many modern issues have some direct biblical connection and are clearly linked to the words and actions of Jesus. But because science as we know it did not exist in New Testament times, we have to test this issue against less specific words and actions. There seem to be obvious links between many Gospel stories and the physical, social and mental state of those who today might benefit from further research. The disabled and others who suffer are often relatively poor, and feel vulnerable, even excluded – the very people Jesus centres on in his teaching and healing. But for many Christians the debate centres rather on the origin of life, with widely varying understandings of what the Creation stories mean for today. As summarised in 'Changing Lives', this is about the extent of authority given to us by God. As with assisted suicide, it is about the level of intervention that we should be allowed – should we leave it all to God?

Free vote?

Much of the pre-Parliamentary debate was around allowing a free vote. This was seen by Denis Macshane, a former government minister, to undermine the reason for the Houses of Parliament to exist:

I respect the Catholic and other religions, just as I respect CND and Liberty, but if every difficult issue with ethical implications is a matter for free votes, then democracy, Parliament, and the purposes of government become meaningless. [5]

The free-vote issue added to the dilemma already made difficult by requests for changes in the law on abortion which would dominate discussion. Government ministers and other MPs, apart from some Roman Catholics, tried to concentrate on whether the human embryology part of the bill was practical as well as ethical. This was put well by Alan Johnson, the then Health Secretary:

For people suffering from Parkinson's disease and motor neurone disease, this is not a question of some issue about the procedure through the House of Commons. This is an issue about whether we can find the drugs that can cure their illnesses. So this is the heart of the matter.

The Liberal Democrat Evan Harris, speaking as a member of the Commons Innovation, Universities, Science and Skills Select Committee, believed the research should be allowed if it 'might be used to treat people with incurable diseases'. Other MPs were more committed to the idea of the free vote; Stephen Pound was one: 'We seem to be moving into a sphere where we are actually taking on the role of the creation of life.'

The free-vote idea was both initiated and given support by Church leaders. The Roman Catholic Archbishops of England, Scotland and Wales all spoke out and also urged MPs, Roman

[5] This and following quotes sourced from personal web sites and collectively on www.bbc.co.uk/news

Catholics especially, to vote 'freely'. The Archbishop of Wales wrote to the Prime Minister, requesting the free vote because this touched on *'the sacredness of human life, its meaning and purpose'*. It was obvious that they expected this vote, once free of party preferences, to go against the motion – conscience could only drive people in one direction.

Tony Blair's speech dealt with community values but it would be interesting to know how this convert to Roman Catholicism would have voted had he still been in office. The argument in favour of a free vote was linked to the idea that ethical issues should be based on non-Party criteria. However, are not many issues such as peace, community and almost everything, from taxation to terrorism, also ethical issues? Returning to Denis Macshane,

> *MPs are also ethically challenged by decisions to go to war, to vote for nuclear weapons, or on issues like ID cards or length of detention before charges.*

The religious debate

In his 2008 Easter sermon the Anglican Bishop of Durham linked human embryology to other issues,

> *The irony is that this secular utopianism is based on a belief in an unstoppable human ability to make a better world, while at the same time it believes that we have the right to kill unborn children and surplus old people, and to play games with the humanity of those in between.* [6]

---

[6] http://www.ntwrightpage.com/sermons/EasterDay08.htm

I might argue that, if no research is allowed, I could feel I was being abandoned like one of those 'surplus old people'. He does not make clear what 'games' are being played with humanity.

The most publicized argument against the Bill came in a 2009 sermon by Cardinal O'Brien:

> *The norm has always been that children have been born as the result of the love of man and woman in the unity of a marriage. That belief has of course long been challenged. However I believe that a greater challenge than that even faces us the possibility now facing our country is that animal human embryos be produced with the excuse that perhaps certain diseases might find a cure from these resulting embryos...With full might of government endorsement, Gordon Brown is promoting a Bill that will allow the creation of animal-human hybrid embryos. He is promoting a Bill which will add to the 2.2 million human embryos already destroyed or experimented upon. He is promoting a Bill allowing scientists to create babies whose sole purpose will be to provide, without consent of anyone, parts of their organs or tissues. He is promoting a Bill which will sanction the raiding of dead peoples' tissue to manufacture yet more embryos for experimentation. He is promoting a Bill which denies that a child has a biological father, allows tampering with birth certificates, removing biological parents, and inserting someone altogether different. And this Bill will indeed be used to further extend the abortion laws...It is difficult to imagine a single piece of legislation which more comprehensively attacks the*

sanctity and dignity of human life than this particular Bill.[7]

The same argument is used in the anti-abortion debate and in the Roman Catholic Church's condemnation of condoms. Life must occur naturally and not be prevented in any way. The creation of life can be planned in a natural way through abstinence or avoiding sexual contact at monthly times of possible fertility, but not by human-designed intervention. (A former Archbishop of Westminster had spoken differently on contraception; while agreeing with O'Brien on abortion, contraception was acceptable if the conscience was clear. I somehow doubt he would have said the same in this debate, but it is an interesting speculation). The conventional view is that life cannot be destroyed once created and it should not be realised artificially. Some people (including those fighting HIV/AIDS, and the victims of rape) argue that the creation of life in certain circumstances is inhuman but many Christians would still not want any life to be ended. Indeed, for them it is clear and simple, avoids complicated debate, is consistent in its practice and, above all, has a core value in its origin.

This 'origin' has to do with the sanctity of human life which, since it comes from God, is not something humans can interfere with. This is the clear basis of the argument, though it was interesting that the Cardinal's sermon did not make direct references to any theology of life. His words were in the context of an Easter message which went on to encourage his listeners to be missionaries; as such they must speak out on Christian principles.

The principles spoken of in the sermon are 'human rights, human dignity and human life' and the proposed change is a

---

[7] The Daily Record, 23 March 2008

'monstrous attack' on all three. But it is here that the logic becomes difficult, because those three can themselves be in conflict. Human dignity might be seen to be under threat if this proposal were allowed (though its proponents would say the opposite) but what about the human dignity of the child rape victim? Is not the dignity of an abused child who is denied abortion more important than that of a yet-to-mature foetus? The Cardinal did not mention how the Church should deal with major denials of these three principles in such areas as war or preventable poverty (though that criticism might be defended as unfair in an obviously focussed sermon).

Linking the argument to human dignity does not take it forward – but what about human rights? I might argue that to deny a possible prevention or cure for MND is an attack on my own human rights. And does not the partner of an AIDS victim have the right to use a condom to prevent not only their own infection but also the possible birth of an infected child?

Neither human dignity nor human rights seemed to be an issue for those who exhumed and patched up the body of Padre Pio (who died around forty years ago and was one of the many sanctified by the late Pope John Paul II). Some people see this as an opportunity to revere a miracle-maker of the twentieth century; others ask what right we have to disturb human remains for anything other than a criminal investigation. Dignity and rights depend very much on personal opinions.

O'Brien's linking of the sanctity of human life to rights and dignity is unfortunate if it implies all three are of equal importance. If so, then human life cannot be advocated either alongside or over and against human rights or dignity. I suspect that his sentence linking the three was more a useful crowd-pleaser than strict logic, so we have to return to 'human life' and its sanctity.

Some Muslim teaching on this is in many ways similar to the more traditional Christian beliefs. While the Shia minority would agree with the Cardinal, the Sunni majority only disagree within themselves about whether the Qur'an suggests 40 or 120 days after conception before real and complete life begins. They therefore have no problem with these embryology research proposals. The Christian tradition was, until quite recently, the same. While reciting the Prayer Book creed I learned as a child, I remember choirboys whose hands would become cowboy guns when we got to 'the quick and the dead'. The boyhood link to Saturday Westerns apart, the real meaning of the phrase is to do with the beginning of life. It was believed that life began when the unborn child first kicked; women could not be hanged if pregnant and the child was 'alive' in that way.

We can argue that we have developed a deeper understanding of life since the writing of that Creed in 325AD, and now say 'the living and the dead', but there is no definition of the 'living'. It is clearly easier to take a view that 'life' must always be given the same importance, but is it real 'life' if a human skin cell is put for a maximum of fourteen days into an egg from another creature with which there is no union?

Adam and Eve – God and therapeutic cloning?

The crux of the matter is that there should be no intervention in the creating of life, yet in the western world most Christians practice birth control and even Roman Catholic women are permitted to test their bodies to avoid times when intercourse might produce pregnancy – a subtle difference from contraception, but still intervention and deliberate prevention. Sexual intercourse does not stop when women can no longer bear children – indeed for many, once the menopause is over, it is something of a liberation. There are donor implants and in vitro fertilisation. People choose the bits of life in which they feel they can intervene.

Alan Billings, who lectures in ethics at Lancaster University, spoke of something at the very centre of all this on a Radio 4 Thought for the Day in March 2008.[8] In the biblical account of human beginnings the very first woman to be created is fashioned from one of Adam's ribs – which Billings pointed out 'sounds astonishingly like a bit of therapeutic cloning'.

That story is considered to be myth by many modern Christians – it did not really happen that way; evolution is much more 'natural'. But while that Old Testament story can be dismissed, another from the New Testament is much more central for most believers. Billings puts this in a wider context:

> *One of the more curious aspects of Christianity is the contrast between the way God is sometimes thought to act in the world and the way some theologians think we should act. God cuts across nature – as Christians are reminded today, the feast of the Annunciation. Mary is told by the angel that she will give birth to a child without the agency of a man, without sex. Yet – according to these theologians – we must always allow nature to take its course; we must never intervene to enable a pregnancy, or to prevent one.*

Traditional theologians will no doubt argue that this was the finest thing that ever happened to a woman, and that to be

---

[8] Alan Billings, *Thought for the day*, BBC Radio 4, 31 March 2008

chosen by God for this purpose was honour rather than abuse, but maybe Mary's strange position as a 'chosen victim' was one reason why she was doctrinally almost removed from the human life cycle at her own birth and in her 'Assumption' (this is dealt with in more detail in Chapter 8, 'Back to the Beginning'). If it is acceptable to place a divine presence in a human body for eternity, surely it can be permitted to place a human cell in an animal egg for less than a fortnight?

Sanctity of life

Alan Billings held that the debate centred on two issues – the sanctity of life and 'fear of playing God'. I have already dealt with the first of these in part, but before moving on to that second theme it is worth adding Billing's comparison of the different levels of importance that should be accorded to an acorn and an oak tree. To treat a mature human being (the oak tree) in the same way as a few cells (the acorn) is for him 'a failure in discrimination'. Not a very exact parallel, as an acorn is considerably more developed than the permitted fourteen-day cells. But seeing a wonderful ancient oak tree compared with hundreds of acorns, most of which will be eaten and few, if any, develop into mature trees, is helpful when thinking of 'sanctity'. For humans, not concerned with eating acorns, the tree's beauty certainly gives it greater value.

I would add to that argument the very personal parallel of the 5,000 people in the UK currently dying of Motor Neurone Disease. They (and I) might not be beautiful but we have value and, in Billings' words, we have sanctity too which is being denied in the argument against research. While a counter-argument about an eventual place in heaven making up for any suffering we have here can be comforting to some, to therefore outlaw research into human disease is to me as theologically unacceptable as ignoring the plummeting life expectancy in Zimbabwe or restoring the excluded verse from 'All things Bright and Beautiful' which says that 'God made them high and lowly'. The value and quality of human life **are** part of its sanctity – and once again, it is the commands and example of Jesus that should guide us: no-one is excluded, the vulnerable need help and the old ways are not good enough (see Chapter 8, 'Back to the Beginning').

Fear of playing God

So what of the 'fear of playing God'? We do it all the time. Often we fail to keep Jesus' commands or follow his example; although that is the task we are given. In this particular case it is clear that 'old ways' do not deal with this issue directly at all but, as always, there are fundamental biblical passages that are still relevant and from which we can find clues to our modern dilemmas. In the fraught issue of the 'truth' of the creation stories in Genesis, I take the side of those who believe their central point is that human beings are given the responsibility of making decisions as well as control over creation. In the New Testament the promise is made that we will be continually guided by God's presence in the Holy Spirit. Analysing the first and last parts of the Bible is a way of attempting to discover what is right, but our responsibilities are still not easy and we can clearly make wrong and selfish decisions. I believe the right decisions are those that fit the commands and example of Jesus in dealing with the vulnerable and excluded. The example of Jesus outweighs the views of those who believe God gave us no power to make 'life' decisions. Even they would surely agree that Jesus is God and that his words and deeds relate much more closely than the creation myths to the kind of decisions we should make. In the way the research is planned, no-one is vulnerable and many of the excluded will benefit. MND sufferers are a tiny minority of those who might benefit – it is hoped to find cures for diseases and genetic disorders which include Parkinson's, muscular dystrophy and cancer.

Promote research – Church of England view

Had it not been seen in the media as yet another blunder by Gordon Brown in the way he treated dissent within his own party, this debate would have faded away much faster. No such publicity was given to a report I was then pleased to discover; one religious group within British Christianity had already considered the issue and taken a different attitude. The Mission and Public Affairs Council of the Church of England responded to the proposal in June 2007, long before it was due to come to Parliament. It concluded that other possible research methods should be promoted and recognised the natural anxieties that people would have, but also gave approval – with two provisos:

> *While we fully support the discovery of means of alleviating presently untreatable diseases, we are concerned that unrealistic expectations may cause distress and disappointment to sufferers. The impression should not be given that the only route towards stem cell therapies is through the use of cytoplasmic hybrids. Rather, work on the isolation and differentiation of adult stem cells should be encouraged. Furthermore, the elucidation of the mechanism by which a differentiated*

cell is dedifferentiated when placed in an enucleated egg cell should lead to our being able to produce embryonic stem cells from already differentiated cells thus circumventing the formation of CNR embryos for this purpose.

Many Christians who accept the creation of embryonic stem cells by CNR using only human material feel deeply uncomfortable about creating cytoplasmic hybrids even for research up to 14 days. Given the dubious efficacy of this research and its controversial nature, some assurance should be given to those who are concerned about this development. Our support for this work going ahead has two added provisos.

First, that there is not an unending commitment to using embryos in this way but rather a limitation on the issuing of licences for such research to a period of say five years. If it is shown in this period that little progress can be made using cytoplasmic hybrids, it would signal a genuine commitment to upholding the status of the embryo as defined in law if such licences were then no longer allowed to be issued.

Secondly, we would like to see the Government state an intention that if research into the dedifferentiation of differentiated cells is successful, licences will not be issued for using embryos to obtain embryonic stem cells once these can be derived from differentiated cells. [9]

In the only specifically Christian reference, the Council mentions the scriptural distinctiveness of all creatures, the uniqueness of humans created in God's image and prohibitions

---

[9] www.england.anglican.org/media/45705/humantissue.pdf

about bestiality. None of this traditional understanding of human creation affects their conclusion, though it does mean that hybrids should not be allowed to develop. The supportive Anglican bishop of Swindon has explained why the fourteen-day limit is required – until that time it is impossible even to know if the growth would lead to single or multiple foetuses, so research should be limited to that 'pre-recognition' period.

Research should therefore, in the report's conclusion, be allowed for a specific period, but they believe that this will be an intermediate process and that the non-human egg will not always be needed. This sensible approach was confirmed in 2009 by advances in stem cell research which will no doubt be furthered by the change in USA policy. President Obama both permitted and promised funding for stem cell and other related research.

In addition to its scientific and ethical decisions, the Council also recognises that, perhaps just as crucial to final decisions and certainly to public opinion, is possible repugnance. This

> *'yuk' factor is neither a final arbiter of acceptability nor necessarily the artefact of unscientific and uneducated thought. Rather it reminds us to pause and consider carefully where the appropriate boundaries should lie and to seek wisdom to do so.*

Principles

This is a debate in which little biblical material can be used. Even those who believe the beginning of life happened according to one of the biblical creation stories would find it hard to make a direct link to human embryology research – and their arguments can be countered, as by Alan Billings. Our conclusion has to be based much more on the understanding we have of the way Jesus would want us to act, even though, with the intervention of two thousand years of scientific understanding, there are no biblical verses to be plucked out.

We have to embrace all the love that Jesus advocated and must give priority to the excluded and vulnerable. I would therefore argue that creating temporary human cells without harming anybody, possibly leading to major changes in the lives of individuals and their families, enhances rather than denies the sanctity of life.

A quite different argument against it is that we should give priority to research in solving far more common illnesses – the obvious one being malaria. That is an argument against this research that I might advocate if I did not suffer from MND myself – but I can think of no other.

It is worth quoting those words of Richard Harries again:

> *... for us human beings it would be unnatural just to let nature to take its course. That is what happens with the birds and the bees, but we are different. We have rational minds, and wills to choose. What is natural for us is that we use the minds God has given us to interact with natural processes in order to enhance human well-being.* [10]

So thank you Parliament for sticking to what I believe Jesus would have advocated had he been preaching to us two thousand years later.

---

[10] Rt. Rev Lord Richard Harries, BBC Thought for the Day, 31 Oct 2008

LIFE IN THE BALANCE

One night some months after diagnosis I had a strange experience. Lying flat on the back can sometimes produce breathing problems for people with MND and in bed my breathing was getting very weak. Suddenly it became quicker and slightly heavier (symptoms which, I have read, often appear close to the point when breathing finally ceases). At the same time I began to see a bright light – even with my eyes closed it seemed as if strong lights had been turned on in the room. Most of us have heard stories of those brought back from death who describe experiences of going into a tunnel of bright light and then (often disappointingly) returning to a very different life and light.

I have to admit that I was frightened rather than looking forward to a life beyond death. My fear was about death when not prepared, not having put things right in my life, and above all not having said goodbye to the most important person in my life, lying next to me. On later reflection, I did not see this as a religious experience but rather something doctors could explain as a symptom associated with weakness.

Life is not something I will experience much longer, which is why I have been facing questions which I have never had the time (or perhaps the reason) to confront before. Though many Christians find their suffering is eased in some way by their faith, it is neither caused nor prevented by God. Similarly, God does not divinely select the time we die.

Over the years I have had good fortune in escaping death several times. I travelled a lot in my twelve years with USPG, and every year I would go to the Caribbean or Latin America via New York in order to first meet with those in the USA Episcopal Church who had similar regional responsibility to mine. I always caught the last trans-Atlantic flight from Heathrow, which was then operated by Pan Am. I was booked on the Lockerbie disaster flight, but changed my plans a few days before.

Most normal weekdays I used to commute from Southampton to London on the train which got me into the USPG offices well before most London-based colleagues. One day I decided to work first from home; my usual train crashed, people were killed and many injured. Many familiar faces were never seen on the platform again, some because they could not face using that particular train.

On the day of the 7 July London bombing I was on my way to Heathrow to meet with an Irishman I had recruited, who was in transit en route to a Methodist-run project in Nigeria. I left home with Gaby, who worked in a similar job to me but at the Methodist headquarters near Baker Street underground station. I planned to go on from there to catch the Heathrow Express from Paddington Station. Waiting on Baker Street platform, we were all told that the system was closing down. I later learned that the train just in front of mine had been blasted by a suicide bomber.

Cats are supposed to have nine lives. I am getting close if we add in two motor accidents, one caused by me. Though they affected me much more than the near-misses above, I hardly think of them, and was remarkably calm on each occasion. The first was in Namibia. I had driven two black priests from the capital, Windhoek, to a mining compound way out in the countryside (fancy having a white chauffeur under apartheid!). I paid a call on the white mine owners and then joined the priests. The compound seemed more like a prison, with crowded 'cells' full of concrete bunks, no mattresses or cupboards for anything personal. The men were not allowed out except to the mine. They would all have left their families in their black 'bantustan' (probably Ovamboland, where later I was a teacher). This was in the white-only part of the country, so they had no right to go elsewhere to search for a better job.

It gets dark very quickly in Namibia. We were driving back on a fairly major road which, like nearly every road, was just scraped out of the ground with gravel added where needed. It would be called a 'dirt road'. In the dark I was driving round a gradual left bend uphill, lights shining into the sky. Suddenly the road turned back on itself to go downhill. I tried to turn the car, but being a Volkswagen beetle, the engine was at the back, so it slid round on the loose gravel two or three times and eventually hit the rock on one side of the road (better than the other side, which would have rolled us down the hill). The top of the car was bent in as if the roof had been put on upside down. A lorry drove past but did not stop, probably because of the black faces. The engine was still going so we squeezed in and drove back to Windhoek, slightly hunched up.

Even more serious was when we were driving back to London from a holiday near St. Ives. We were going uphill and there was a steep downhill slope to our left. On a holiday weekend, traffic was very busy. Suddenly a car coming the opposite way started heading towards us – the driver had fallen asleep. Because of the slope to our left I could not swerve very much but managed to avoid a head-on collision. The outside wing of the car was flattened but far more dangerous was being spun round right in front of the downhill traffic. Luckily, the next driver had had 'advanced driver' training and was keeping a good distance, so we survived unharmed.

That seems like five out of the cat's nine lives. And then I remembered that plane. I was in Guyana to see how the missionaries I was responsible for were doing. Two were in a remote area, responsible for training indigenous people to be priests in their own community. It could take days to get there, through rainforest and across rivers on what were laughingly called roads. So, with a maintenance worker, I boarded a tiny single-engine plane. I sat next to the pilot, who gave us a smooth journey by avoiding clouds. He went round, above or below them and also leaned the plane over at incredible angles so I could take photos. I then had five days of discussions and giving encouragement, sleeping in a hammock to avoid both mosquitoes and snakes.

Flying back was very different. Because both gold and diamonds could be found in the interior, all aircraft had to report to the international airport in Georgetown. We left from the gravel scrape called a runway in mid-afternoon, just as the almost daily tropical storm began. No avoiding cloud this time. We had to follow the same flight path as the international jet I had arrived on the week before. We were soon enveloped in a massive set of bubbling stormy clouds. We spent the next half hour rising and falling, with no view of the ground or clear sky, and the altitude dial whizzing round one way and then the other. The pilot was magnificent and seemed very calm – perhaps he dealt with this every day – but for me it was the longest and most frightening experience I have ever had and the only time when I thought I might not survive.

And then there was the escape from malaria in Mozambique described in the previous chapter. It all adds up to a lot of close escapes; but I never anticipated a slow, debilitating illness.

CHAPTER 12

What now?

What I have explored is a very personal mixture of experience, issues and ideas: some come from other people (selected either because I agree with them or want to show why I do not), all are trying to explain some very personal opinions. Despite what may sometimes seem an attempt to gain sympathy, I have tried to put in perspective what has become important to me as I face death, looking at how I have felt as a result of my illness and the 'suffering' that comes with it.

I believe that to strive for salvation can be selfish, and that we often ignore principles because we are obsessed with rules (observance of which, many people believe, might earn us salvation - as long as we believe the right thing). I have outlined some of the things which I believe Christians should do, using biblical as well as other material. The New Testament is particularly important where it details or expands on first-hand memories of the core teachings of Jesus. Church doctrines are important only when they follow that same path.

Am I really a Christian?

The question that remains is whether or not the faith I still claim is enough for me to be called a Christian, let alone an (admittedly inactive) ordained member of the Anglican Church; not believing in the effect of prayer except as a time to think. I still attend church at least once a week, though I can no longer participate except through listening. Given the nature of my beliefs, why do I bother? Why do I narrow down the importance of Jesus' teaching to ethics and ignore what the same texts say about eternal life? Even in the worldwide church, in which those who hold views at each of the extremes are known for condemning the other, there will be underlying agreement on the basic events of the life of Jesus.

So where am I now? Have I changed my position in doing all this thinking? Reflecting on suffering has not made me hope for a cure. Instead, it has made me think about many aspects of human relationships. If anything, all this analysis has confirmed what I believe, however questionable my logic has been.

All Just Myth?

It has been good to find others who are on a similar path and the free Divinity lectures at Gresham College, which I enjoyed attending before I became ill, have helped. I particularly remember some of those lectures given about ten years ago by Richard Holloway, which also formed the basis of his 2001 book Doubts and Loves. In his lecture Christianity as Myth[1] he says,

> *We look out on life and we look in on ourselves, making both out there and in here the object of our own gaze, our own concern. That act of looking or gazing or being concerned gives rise to 'religion', which means a kind of connection to the mystery of what is beyond ourselves,*

[1] Richard Holloway, Christianity as Myth, Gresham College, 15/11/2000

however we define it. That is why even atheism can be religious, because it is also about that ultimate concern, that final question we ask about ourselves. What we call faith, of one sort or another, is unavoidable here. Faith is our response to that which we cannot establish with certainty. (p.4)

At that point in the lecture he had been discussing the ideas of another theologian, Paul Tillich, of whom he says,

For Tillich the only real atheism was a complete lack of concern for the meaning of our existence: 'Indifference toward the ultimate question is the only imaginable form of atheism.' [2]

Holloway went on to discuss how, as humans, we want more than that. We want our myth to become reality. There are classic Old Testament examples. The Hebrew leaders avoided giving God a name, fearing that some link with a human object would lead to idolatry. And in one sense they were right. In Exodus 32 people are not happy with Moses' version of God, who is not accessible to them and hidden behind clouds. They easily accept Aaron's request to bring gold jewellery to make the golden calf, the image of the God who brought them out of Egypt. Holloway sees that,

idolatry is always a greater danger to religion than atheism, because it identifies something we ourselves have created, something that is essentially an extension

---

[2] Paul Tillich (1958) Dynamics of Faith, Harper Torchbooks, New York, p.45

or projection of ourselves, with that which is beyond our knowing or creating. (p.5)

The need to be in control

Humans have always attempted to put together images of how we would like things to be and, as I certainly feel about the Virgin Mary (Back to the Beginning), these images can sometimes be engineered and used by those who want to influence, even control, our faith. Control is very much part of the cause of the divisions of the church on doctrinal matters, both historically at international level (Orthodox/Catholic division, the formation of the Church of England and all the torture and burnings that resulted from religious difference), and nowadays in petty ways in independent churches.

I came across an example of the 'petty' when visiting an Anglican parish priest on one of the more remote islands in the Bahamas. While I was there, he was visited by two former parishioners who had left to form their own church. They had then fallen out over a sermon one had given and had come back to the priest for an academic resolution. The issue was whether David had written a particular psalm. The continuing disagreement produced another new church which was where 'true' salvation could be guaranteed. The priest suggested to me that there were also probably other hidden motives, including power and respect in the community and even the financial advantage of the traditional ten percent tithe.

Cardinal Murphy O'Connor has a very different outlook to mine. He gave a lecture at Westminster Cathedral in May 2008, the theme being that Britain cannot become a 'God-free Zone'.[3]

---

[3] Report in *The Times*, 09/05/2008

He spoke of both public interest in religion, and a spiritual homelessness in which faith is not seen as an option. He sees religion as privatised and 'a matter of personal need rather than as a truth that makes an unavoidable claim on us'. He suggests there is a sense of loss, of people not being in touch with 'living sources that can nourish them', of wanting to live by shared values but not knowing where to find them. We have impulses and aspirations which are not met or challenged in our present society but at the same time we do not want to commit ourselves to God because to do that is 'to take a step back from being independent and mature'.

Given the authoritarian nature of much church hierarchy – and certainly that of Roman Catholicism – most non-believers would, I suspect, not be happy with being told they should forego their independence, especially as the Cardinal goes on to say that one of the characteristics of his church is 'the stability and strength of its structure as a community held in communion and truth by the Pope and Bishops'. This is underlined by his affirmation of an un-named Muslim theologian who had praised Pope Benedict for understanding 'that religion is about truth and not social cohesion'. His stress on the importance of believing what you are told harks back to my chapter 'Selfish Salvation'. To imply that truth is to believe what you are told and that it does not matter if that affects the way we relate to each other seems to be against the Principles of Jesus which, I suggest, are the core of true faith. To be denied independent thought and to be judged if we strive for 'social cohesion' seems to me highly insulting and not likely to convince people to change their minds.

Is commitment enough?

So the question still remains – why do I stay part of something I seem to disagree with so much? People without any faith in the divine can be independent and mature and may also be highly committed to humanitarian issues and causes, many of which are in harmony or even linked with Christian-backed social programmes. Am I, whether truly mature or not, really just one of them rather than a Christian at all? Or are there just 'levels' of belief? Some words on that idea in a Thought for the Day by the Hindu Akhandadhi Das intrigued me.

> *There is a section of the 12th chapter of the Bhagavad-Gita which offers a rare piece of theological compromise. Often, religious treatises are strong on absolute and non-negotiable pronouncements. But, here's Sri Krishna offering concessions: 'Just fix your mind and intelligence on God without deviation and you will attain the Supreme without doubt. If that's too difficult, follow the principles of devotional service and try to worship and serve God in your daily life. In that way, you will develop deeper spiritual commitment. But, if that's not possible for you, doing God's work will gradually lead you to perfection. If you are unable to do that, then dedicate your wealth for the benefit of others. And, if you can't even do that, then cultivate inner knowledge, because that will inspire you to meditation, to charity and selflessness.* [4]

---

[4] Akhandadhi Das, Thought for the Day, BBC Radio 4, 15/04/2008

I often see myself as part of that theological compromise. I have described myself as a high church Baptist/Methodist/Quaker who, if born as a Sikh, would have remained so. High church, not because of theology but personal history and congregational involvement; Baptist only in that I do not believe infant baptism makes somebody a member without their consent or guarantees heaven; Methodist only because of their left-wing history; Quaker because they have no traditional doctrine, unlike the Church of England's Thirty Nine Articles (even when I was ordained, the radicals were saying they crossed their fingers behind their backs as they took part in the swearing of allegiance to doctrine before ordination). Sikhism attracts because of their respect for other faiths but, above all, their understanding that faith develops as we learn more about God's world and we have to apply the understanding of the ten Gurus to the present day.

The obvious connection is with the Principles I advocate – the key objectives which can be applied to present day situations which would have been inconceivable to New Testament thinkers and writers. If Jesus was truly human, there is no way that he could even dream of the kind of society we now live in. I could have added other faith groups to the above list – I admire the Salvation Army for its commitment to the poor – but none of those I have mentioned are perfect, otherwise I would have joined them.

Returning to that Hindu quote above, I sometimes feel I fit at the end of the list – 'cultivate inner knowledge, because that will inspire you to meditation, to charity and selflessness'. Am I doing God's work, even if I am not a conventional believer? Am I cultivating inner knowledge in the hope that this will lead to meditation, charity and selflessness? The last, at least, I hope is true. I certainly agree that 'often, religious treatises are strong on absolute and non-negotiable pronouncements,' but is the central Christian belief still the notion that God is behind all the good things we do, even if we do not recognise or realise it? If atheists, agnostics, 'heathens', members of non-Christian faiths, heretics and doubters all have the same hidden motivation, how – beyond the selfish hope for salvation – does it help to be an accepted Christian? Is our responsibility just in accepting or rejecting the calls of our consciences which come from God? We all have feelings of conscience, however it is explained. What convinces me less is when people say that God is always behind everything their church says or does. My understanding of what the 'Jesus-form' of God teaches is very different.

The Principles of Jesus do not require me to believe that Jesus is one of the Trinitarian 'forms' of God. He may be, there may be a God – indeed I rather hope there is – but beyond hope there is for me no proven belief. Faith cannot be 'proven': that is the point of the word.

A bit of history

If those are the boundaries of faith for me, why do I still go to church, why do I not see myself as a humanist and find leadership, conviction and Principles in that system? Recalling some of Chapter 5, I need to understand what made me. On one of the rare occasions when the Sunday school I was sent to as a child participated in a service in church, I saw this fantastic thing called a 'choir'. Someone I knew was in it, so could I be too? It turned out that my Sunday school teacher's husband was a tenor in the choir and I was encouraged to join. Coming from a home with no church links and no recorded music (odd, I thought later, since my father had been an army bandsman apparently able to play fourteen instruments), this was my introduction to the kind of music which I later found was called 'classical'. I had learned to read music through violin lessons, so took to singing more easily than many others. The choir dominated my boyhood and youth – until my voice broke even Saturdays were taken up with pocket-money-producing weddings.

In my teenage years I got more involved in liturgy, partly because people were leaving in droves in reaction to a bumbling new incumbent. While most of my working life was in faith-based charities rather than ministry, I never left behind what had been the dominant influence in my upbringing.

A real community

Music was the gateway through which I became part of something more important to my life than anything else. My learning how to relate to people of all ages and backgrounds with many interests and commitments, was fostered in what I later realised was a 'community'. And that community gave me my girlfriends and spouses too.

The church I have been part of for so long chooses to label itself on its website 'The Church of England – a Christian presence in every community'. It was therefore good to hear in June 2008 of a Church report on that 'presence in every community'.[5] Some of the media focussed exclusively on the part of the report which criticised government concentration

---

[5] Church of England Report, Moral, But No Compass – Government, Church and the future of Welfare, 2008

on Muslim communities. In a BBC Radio 4 interview on June 9th, the Bishop of Hulme pointed out that the government held national maps and statistics for Mosques and Muslims but not for the 14,000 Anglican communities in England. While a government minister rightly pointed out that this had more to do with countering extremism, conservative Christian criticism of exclusion from 'community cohesion' continued with claims that attempts to make Muslims and other minority faith communities more integrated by being more sensitive to them had had the opposite effect.

In contrast, on the same day as the Bishop of Hulme interview, The Guardian mentioned neither interfaith issues, nor Islamic ones, but got to the core of the report.[6] It gave a far more neutral and centred view with no hidden agenda, as some of the Christian papers had. It is worth quoting at length:

> *The Archbishops of Canterbury and York will today support the findings of a report criticizing the government for its failure to recognize the Church of England's contribution to the public sphere.*
>
> *'Moral, But No Compass', challenges the government to recognize the church's involvement and potential in reforming public services. Recommendations include appointing a minister for religion and new legislation that does not discriminate against faith-based charities.*
>
> *Rowan Williams and John Sentamu are expected to issue a 'warm welcome' for the findings and call for a sensible dialogue with the government about the role of the church in contemporary British life, especially in the field of welfare services. A team from the Von Hügel Institute at St Edmund's College, Cambridge, approached Church of*

---

[6] Riazatt Butt in The Guardian, 09/05/2008

England bishops, MPs, peers and academics. Participants agreed that the government displayed 'religious illiteracy' and had little or no interest in Christian involvement in civic and charitable work.

The Rt. Rev Stephen Lowe, the Bishop of Hulme, who commissioned the report, said: 'This report raises serious issues about the church and its relationship to the government'.

The report comes in the same week that the government launches a taskforce to improve engagement with faith communities. It will be led by Malcolm Duncan from Faithworks, a cross-denominational Christian group, and will embark on a consultation that will report back in 2009.

While some of the report criticized government and might indicate support for campaigns I disagree with (such as that by evangelical groups to make all their employees – from cleaners to directors – sign a statement of belief), the main issue was around the communities created and supported by the churches throughout the country.

The weekly newsletter at the church I attend had, in a single week, people participating in a hospice sponsored walk, a hog roast to raise money for the homeless, a quiz in aid of the Salvation Army, and reminders of both a quarterly fundraiser for a charity working with stressed farmers and a box for supermarket vouchers for a local school. There was an open garden which was keeping fifty percent of contributions for the church but all the other notices were to do with the wider community – and from a congregation of less than fifty people.

Churches often encompass a wide variety of people of differing talents and intellect. Partly because of mission history, but also through individual links, they also have worldwide connections and interests and many (for example) have Fairtrade stalls. The church I attend now, unlike my previous one, has no members from Africa or elsewhere; however, it is part of a local 'Christian Care for One World' group which, at a recent civic event, had the only stall concerned with the wider world community.

Churches are not all or always so visionary and some use community outreach as a way to gain membership but it is my strong belief that churches have a leading role here, following the Principles of Jesus. It is well known that Christians on average give away a much higher percentage of their income than those without faith. The BBC clearly agrees, as their weekly charity appeal for community-based projects is always sandwiched between their 'Sunday' faith news programme and Sunday Worship. The eclectic congregation at St. Martin in the Fields in London's Trafalgar Square has both a famous choir and a ministry to the homeless which is a model for us all. Sunday services bring together each church community – some people concentrate on music, some on prayer and others look forward to the sermon. The last includes me, since I can no longer join in anything needing speech or singing. But the important underlying thing is community. Individuals may choose anything from evangelical choruses, dancing, waving hands and responding 'yes' to words in prayers or sermons to, at the opposite end, traditional Catholic ritual.

The importance of being, or at least feeling, together was evident in the congregation I worshipped with for over ten years in south east London. Ninety percent were black families, some Caribbean but predominantly West African. Despite being from an evangelical part of the Anglican Church, the African part of the congregation chose a 'high' church which did things they had never seen and did not understand; for example, incense was used (any mid-week festivals, including Holy Week, would be largely attended by Caribbean people as they came from a different tradition). The Africans chose this church because they were welcomed, not because of any style of belief or theological nicety. The whole congregation, including me, was held together by common causes; families enjoying their children being with them and finding the worship itself stimulating – including the odd sermon by me. I was there because I wanted to continue to explore my faith and can best do that, then as now, in a community context. I did not and do not find I agree with all words and phrases in liturgy or hymns or other people's sermons but, the latter in particular, make me think through what should be priorities for Christians – or, at least, followers of Jesus.

A Full Circle

As is true for everyone, I am where I am because of a mixture of experiences all the way from childhood to the present. Recalling part of Chapter 5, despite never having done Religious Studies even at 'O' level, I became an ordinand at the age of eighteen and, without knowing its liberal leaning, chose to study theology in the 1960's at King's College in London. It was all new to me and, until fellow students left to go to what I was told were more conservative establishments, I was not really aware of theological differences. I failed the final exams and ended up in Namibia where the newly elected bishop, Colin Winter, made me re-think the purpose of the Church and renewed my urge to be ordained.

I enjoyed many things when working in parishes but, unlike most newly-ordained priests, never wanted to be in charge of one on my own. I always worked in a team, always in a specialist role – college chaplain, youth work and running a Religious Education Centre. This meant I had far less to do with the 'occasional offices' (Baptisms in particular) which highlight belief. Motivated by Colin Winter, preaching was what I most enjoyed. I have even 'preached' once in our local church since coming to live in our new home. Late in 2009 a retired priest who sometimes leads services suggested I write a sermon which he would then read. The Gospel reading was Mark going on about 'the rich', so I could hardly resist that challenge, though it took more than a week to write. I linked the Gospel to the inequalities explored in the book The Spirit Level[7] – a secular 'Blessed are the poor'.

Reflecting on my sermons and on what has been important to me brings me full circle, back to where I first began thinking about writing a book. It has meant I could at last be honest about what I believe – the need to follow the Principles of Jesus, who is acknowledged as the most important leader the world has ever experienced, with more followers than anyone has ever had. That does not mean I claim I am good at being a follower, but that I see those Principles as the key to the survival of our world. Churches are important not because they are a route to 'Selfish Salvation' but because our world needs above all a community – local, national and international – which will carry forward the Principles.

That is my hope for the future of this divided but committed group of people whom we call the 'Church'. Priorities will

---

[7] Richard Wilkinson and Kate Pickett (2009) The Spirit Level, Allen Lane. Explored further in Chapter 2.

certainly need to change. Focusing on the validity or relevance of selected ancient verses of scripture without bringing in other texts and an understanding of their cultural context, leads to concentration on marginal issues. This creates division which serves to dampen the influence of the Church on major issues in the world. This is similar to divisions within governments or political parties, which affect both the making of sensible consensus decisions and the trust of voters. Both Church and politics need to change if they are to make a real difference.

That seems easy to say. It will therefore be easy to criticise me both for contorted logic and to say simply that my lack of faith means I cannot be taken seriously – and that I must therefore be wrong. But if I had left out the Chapter on 'Selfish Salvation' and had not admitted my lack of faith in traditional doctrines, would there be any less criticism? I doubt it.

Despite all I have written here, I have never in my sermons or teaching attacked traditional doctrines. I have not wanted to move people away from what is important to them, as my Real Sermons show.[8] I have advocated Principles rather than rules and also preached against believing for the sake of Salvation. But I am happy that people have confidence in an afterlife – indeed I still have some hope that they may be right, and that there is something to look forward to. I would not attack, but I also would not proclaim, the truth of the Resurrection.

Doing the will of Jesus, replacing old rules with his own Principles, has to be our priority. Our age is very different to that of the New Testament, with more changes in one life-span

---

[8] Some Real Sermons available as downloads from
http://www.gileadbookspublishing.com/when-you-are-dying-additional-chapters.html

than in scores of generations in biblical times. Jesus' Principles are not easy, but they are what he proclaimed. They therefore have to be the priority for Christians if we are to deal with community issues, work for peace or grapple with our relationships with other faiths (that last might seem initially to be purely a faith concern but has links to major international issues). Human embryology may now appear to be an issue which has been dealt with and finished, but the core of the argument will continue as scientists put more possibilities before us. Homophobia clearly occupies my mind both because it is such a divisive issue and because I want to support my many Christian gay friends. But above all, it gives the best example of the need to apply Jesus' Principles to changes in population, priorities and culture (all of which influenced scripture when it was written) and make them the basis of all current decisions. Even if we see scripture as having direct divine origin, we surely cannot ignore the possibility that the Holy Spirit – a manifestation of God's presence – might guide us now.[9] Whether I follow that traditional view or my own, the result is the same - Principles, not rules.

---

[9] Christians and Other Faiths, Community, Peace and Homophobia all available as downloads from
http://www.gileadbookspublishing.com/when-you-are-dying-additional-chapters.html

CHAPTER 13

Hope

I hope I am wrong – not about Principles, but about what happens after death. I don't want never to be with Gaby again. I suspect I am not alone in not being terribly happy at Jesus' suggestion that relationships will be so different in the 'after life' that it will not matter how many spouses someone has had (Mt. 22:28). It would be wonderful to have renewed good relations with everyone but, though she is my third wife, I want something special with Gaby. Apart from that, and the thought of doing nothing except continually falling on my knees to worship God, as parts of the book of Revelation suggest, a continued life beyond this world is certainly something I would look forward to. Just like the Biblical writers, I have no idea what actually happens beyond death but, unlike them, I have no heavenly vision.

Meanwhile, a few years more life in this world would help, as long as it has some quality. The Motor Neurone Disease Association (MNDA), through its website and magazine, naturally presents positive stories of how people still manage to enjoy sport, holidays, daily events and cope with specific disabilities. While not ignoring the terminal nature of the disease, the writers generally emphasise a future of some kind to look forward to – at least in this world. I have only met two other people with MND; one who'd had the disease for fifteen years, in a wheelchair but still able to speak, the other for three years, still able to live alone and walk with a stick. If I were one of them I would certainly be much more positive about my future – my physical condition is much worse than either of them. I have also met a widow whose husband died within seven months of diagnosis. The average life expectancy after diagnosis, according to the statistics, is fourteen months; on my computer diary I begin each entry with the number of days I have achieved beyond that.

My feelings about my present life do change. I used to see a neurologist every sixteen weeks and had not expected to be around for the next appointment. Then we agreed that there was little he could add to advice given by my GP and the local hospice. I now feel I will be around for a little longer. The most likely end is deterioration of my breathing muscles, which has already begun and which makes me increasingly sleepy. When I cry (which I do frequently in response to anything reminding me of events in my past or stories of others who have died) my eyebrows drop so that the computer, which needs to 'see' my eyes, will not work. Yawning has the same effect. The crucial question for me is what I am able to achieve as my abilities lessen – typing a line of this text, even when I am fully awake, takes at least fifteen minutes but usually much longer (some parts of this book were written in the early months when things were much easier).

There are times when I have said to myself, 'let me die in peace while asleep', and I have explained previously that I have a Living Will, which means I will be allowed to die if I get another serious condition. But the death-wish changes and sometimes seems to have links with the particular drugs I am on at the time; any kind of opiate seems to make me more depressed and sleepy, and also increases some other weaknesses. My feelings are also linked to the arrival of any new piece of equipment; it may temporarily help mobility but its psychological effect is downwards because, whatever problem it solves, it heralds something else that I will never be able to do again.

A powerful example of the realisation of never being 'able to do again' came when I found myself sobbing uncontrollably at a concert in aid of the local hospice in which Gaby was singing. Another time, less immediately understandable, was at a local food fair where I began sobbing while watching some children playing. It was my inability to be part of anything any more plus, in both cases, realising that they might be the last such occasions. It is like that when I see friends or relatives – is this the last time? And crying is the only way I can react emotionally, even at the pleasure of seeing Gaby smiling and enjoying herself outside her full-time care for me.

And then there are the dreams – or are they fantasies? In my dozing time, usually before falling asleep for my two hour afternoon rest, I sometimes see myself in a pulpit – usually St. Paul's Cathedral in London with a massive congregation. The dream is no doubt linked to my enjoyment of preaching and, even, that I fancy myself as being good at it. But the context is my 'hope'. It is a year since I recovered from MND, and I can both climb the pulpit steps and talk. The reason I have been invited to preach, and why so many have turned up, is that what has happened is a miracle.

I did actually pray on several occasions to be cured – something I have denied the validity of for years (see Chapter 3, Suffering – the Reality). My name is on the prayer list at the church we attend each Sunday. I am exactly like the people I criticise – asking God to help only when there is a personal crisis and not prioritising other people (psychologists would no doubt have plenty to say about that). The thing which I dream to have happened is that which I have spent much time denying – miracle, the power of intercessory prayer and the intervention of God in individuals' lives. If God has such control over our lives, as many claim, does he then ignore the millions who ask for relief? (Chapter 4, Suffering - the Biblical Theory, deals with this in more detail.)

In my dream sermon I do not deny my cure is a miracle (the congregation smiles, some shout 'Hallelujah'). There is, after all, no medical explanation. The specialists are as baffled as everyone else. I am happy to use the term 'miracle' for events that have no explanation, but then I disappoint people because, for me, it has nothing to do with selective divine intervention, whether or not prompted by prayer. The illogicality of change as a result of prayer has always been with me – in current times, why should I be favoured when I have already reached twice the age of the average Zimbabwean? While my hero Desmond Tutu said that apartheid would not survive because millions were praying for change, my own view is that, if prayer has any effect, it is because time is given to thinking through what action we should take in our own lives – and it is that which can have personal, family and even global implications.

I will never know how this dream sermon finished. I either woke up or went into deeper sleep, and it does not seem to happen any more. But what happened while I was awake is even more bizarre. I sat one day trying to think through again my views on prayer and healing. Even if I didn't believe in miraculous healing, let alone in the resurrection of the one who healed all those people in the Gospels, would it work? I stared at a lovely colourful wooden crucifix from Guatemala on the wall above my computer and mentally said 'Ask, I can'. For some weeks I occasionally and almost embarrassingly tried to say the same words out loud, though I could not make the sounds that related to any of it. Once I nearly got my tongue in the right place in my mouth for the 'n' of 'can'. Later on, when again I contravened my own beliefs about praying to be cured, my fingers began to move. In fact, it was probably just part of the continuing decline of my muscles which jerk and judder from time to time even though the motor neurones do not work. But I told myself to stop all this nonsense; if I were a 'true believer' then it would make some sense – but I am not.

In New Testament terms, faith itself is not always essential to apparent cure (see Chapter 4, Suffering - the Biblical Theory). But even that cannot change reality for me. Miracle healing is against all I have argued throughout these pages. My future should not be and will not be dictated by some illogical, unethical and arbitrary intervention.

Prayer has been the centre of my argument so far. It was obviously important to me at certain moments in recent years, but do I apply the same test to other aspects of faith? Do I perceive Christianity and other faiths in those terms: illogical, unethical and arbitrary?

Illogical?

All faiths are illogical, otherwise they would not be 'faiths'; they would be 'proofs'. Christianity preaches a Trinitarian God, which most unbelievers find impossible, though it may explain why Christianity convinced so many Africans whose traditional faiths are largely monotheistic but often see God in a variety of manifestations. Hindus also are not put off by the idea, and some temples have pictures of Jesus on their walls as one way of seeing God. Christian believers have no problem - at least in theory. We believe in Jesus as God while the 'Father' continues to be in control of Creation; but Jesus has also to be fully human, otherwise his achievement of 'sinlessness' is due solely to God's power. Christians, who need to claim God's approval, whether over major things such as the founding of denominations or minor matters in petty arguments, have the Holy Spirit as divine guidance.

I remember a training meeting for the newly-ordained, in a diocese where preaching for such novices was limited to once a month; we enquired how many of us had been given the task on Trinity Sunday and the answer was eight out of ten. Was this a test of our theological depth or perhaps were our parish priests pleased that somebody else was around to tackle this issue? In a later parish I had to prepare youngsters for Confirmation and I found a way to explain the doctrine: H_2O is a single compound but present as water, ice and steam. How this represents the Trinity is maybe acceptable to twelve year olds back in the 1970's, but is hardly an adequate way for believers to explain their faith in things which cannot be proven. Doctrine and physical parallels are irrelevant. Faith needs nothing else except faith – which hardly convinces unbelievers.

Unethical?

Certainly not! That would be the claim of most believers – at least about their own version of faith. They may accuse other faiths of unethical doctrine or practice: some Muslims will regard Christianity as unethical because parts of the Church accept both women and homosexuals as equals; some Christians would accuse Muslims of precisely the opposite. Yet many Christians and Muslims are in conflict among themselves; internal divisions are obvious, particularly over war and justified violence. Within Judaism also there are internal divisions around the occupation of Palestine. Ethical issues are particularly important in elections in the USA, where churches which are opposed to each other on so many issues – especially Roman Catholics and Evangelicals – are agreed in their position on abortion. The country is said to have the highest percentage of practicing Christians in the developed world, yet is also the most unequal. The difficult debate on health care for their poor and lack of care for their unemployed suggests that personal success is more important than helping the vulnerable. However, this 'Prosperity Gospel', linked in my mind to 'Selfish Salvation', is not true of all Christians, any more than all but a tiny minority of Muslims support suicide bombing. There are many thousands of faith-based charities; committed believers give away a greater proportion of their income than those of no faith and many individuals take extraordinary risks in leading campaigns and protests.

Recent ethical dilemmas in the UK include the Pope's intervention, inviting Church of England clergy who disapprove of their own church's move towards the consecration of women bishops to move to the Catholic Church. Likewise the UK Government's intention to prevent religious groups from discriminating against, for example, homosexual teachers in faith schools, which Anglican bishops in the House of Lords supported. The internal argument in the Roman Catholic Church in Ireland over sexual abuse by priests, following similar revelations in Canada and the USA, is an unfortunate example of not only bad personal behaviour but of cover-up by church authorities – certainly unethical.

Most people would agree that suicide-bombing has no religious foundation, but there might be disagreement about assisted suicide, and certainly about the murder of a doctor who carried out abortions. Members of all faiths are largely 'ethical', though disagreeing on specific issues. Bishop Tom Butler, in a Thought for the Day at the time of an Anglican Church General Synod full of controversial issues, suggested that the Anglican Church resembled a herd of animals constantly moving to find nourishment and made up of different species, families and individuals, giving community, safety in numbers and protection from predators.[1]

Chapter 6, Selfish Salvation, criticises any who believe that correct faith is all that matters, and that therefore very few will be 'saved'. Many groups within all faiths would claim they have got the only access to heaven. This reminds me of a story: a Christian of one denomination was wandering round the beautiful forests of heaven when he saw a massive wall he had been unaware of until that moment. He asked St. Peter what this was for and was told there were many such walls, separating faiths, denominations and pagans so that each could assume they alone had 'got it right'. The only group in heaven who wanted to question others was the surprised group of ethical atheists. Nice story, which might give me hope – except that it is just a story.

Arbitrary?

I recently met someone who was planning both a service of renewal of marriage vows and a separate baptism for one of her grandchildren. She knew the vicar because they lived in the same village but, apart from similar family occasions, she never went to church – even at Christmas or Easter. How different is she from me? She may have a more conventional faith than I do, but finds that attending church does not help

[1] Bishop Tom Butler, BBC Thought for the Day, 9th February 2010

her. There may be other obvious reasons for wanting these church ceremonies, including superstition and family unity. Will she go to heaven despite all this? She has been under-paid and over-worked for all her working life. Does following the Principles of Jesus without knowing them or worshipping him count against her?

Several years ago I had an interesting talk with a senior member of another denomination who did not believe in the Resurrection of Jesus. Will this person go to heaven despite this? Will his position in the church be seen as deception or simply as respecting the views of the majority while getting on with work which benefits the wider community? Churches are divided over the acceptance of same-sex relationships. Will those on either side go to heaven despite this?

Some say our future is predestined. For me this cannot mean that, whatever we do or don't do, our future is guaranteed, but a God who knows everything therefore knows all that we will be and do – and what my next sentence will be (scary, I wish I did!).

What comes next?

After all that, what do I believe happens at the end of life? It has not changed, despite wondering each night whether I will be alive in the morning. It never concerned me throughout my life whether there would be anything after death – there were always things which were more important to me. I was asked by a prison chaplain I know to write the 2010 Easter sermon for him to read out to the prisoners. The resurrection reading was from St John, which tells the story of Mary Magdalene at the tomb. As she was a former sinner who loved God, it was an obvious favourite for prisoners but I also included a mention of how difficult it is for me and many others to believe the story:

> *Don't be worried if you're not totally convinced by all bits of the story. The first believers came slowly to their belief. Jesus was not the first or last to claim to be the Messiah, the Son of God. The disciples had the wonderful experience of three years with Jesus, and yet it only slowly dawned on them what had happened. Some of us may have been lucky, totally convinced by the story. Many more, including me, will be hoping it is true. We would love to realise the power and the truth of the risen Christ almost in an instant. We would hope to see the light. For most of us that doesn't happen – it is a gradual growing and understanding, just as it was for the disciples. However far you are along the path to realising what really happened, don't worry because most of the rest of us are stuck there with you.*
>
> *The most important part of the story of the Resurrection is that the first evidence, the first person who had the courage to go to the tomb, as we heard in the gospel today, was not a leader, not a person who had total life innocence, not one of the chosen twelve. It was Mary Magdalene, who was known to have been a sinner, but also who loved Jesus the most. A lesson for us all.* [2]

We attached the sermon to our Easter email update to friends and family and it was the uncertainty I expressed which relieved at least one friend whose beliefs I echoed.

---

[2] The complete sermon is available as a download from http://www.gileadbookspublishing.com/when-you-are-dying-additional-chapters.html

I was thinking through how to end this final and largely negative chapter. Why is the church not following the commands of Jesus? My clergy pension was recently due to be revised; the Church of England announced a new policy of not investing in companies where the differential between the lowest and highest wage packets was more than a factor of 75. I already knew that they did not invest in tobacco companies and others with questionable ethics but I was amazed to hear that the exploitation of the poor had never been part of their agenda before. The policy may reduce my pension but surely most clergy would be equally appalled that the issue of gross inequality had not been addressed long ago.

Yet in spite of all my doubts, questions and criticisms, I still have hope. I hope I am wrong about life after death, though in the eyes of some Christians I would be ineligible for heaven. I hope they are wrong and I hope I am wrong!

For a free download of additional chapters written by Philip Wetherell visit:

http://www.gileadbookspublishing.com/when-you-are-dying-additional-chapters, or scan the following QR Code:

APPENDIX A

Additional notes for Chapter 8, Back to the Beginning

Later sections of Mark's Gospel have a similar pattern of *story* sequence with important *initiative* and *response* sections, with chapter 10 – the story of Jesus' journey from Galilee to Jerusalem – being a transition. This includes a healing and a prediction of death, but also has three crucial events, all of which are responses to situations he is presented with. The first is the need to receive as children do (10:13-16). Second, meeting the rich man who keeps all the Commandments in a technical sense and is undoubtedly a man of great faith, but who is told he will only reach eternal life if he goes one stage further; he has to understand what was behind the Commandments – the Principle rather than the rules – and give up his wealth (10:17-31). Mark has Jesus then immediately referring for the third time to his own death, to which the disciples' response is a question of who will be seated at the right or left hand (10:35-5). Jesus deals with this third event in the same way. Being a disciple on its own no more guarantees salvation and recognition than the rich man's keeping of the commandments. It needs much more than that. The greatest will become the least; even the Son of Man came to serve.

In this section it seems Jesus has decided to confront those who want his end – and this fact is made obvious to his followers for the third time. But the three recorded challenges in this part of the journey were refuted because they were selfish demands. Exclude others because we are closer to you (does that have inter-faith or denominational parallels today?); tell us that rule-keeping is sufficient; and give precedence because of faith in the person rather than through service to those at the bottom of the pile. The response is summed up in the famous words in 10:43, 'The greatest will become the least'. Rather than thinking we have the answers, we are to stop thinking of ourselves. The three themes established in chapter 2 are again dealt with in sequence, beginning with the vulnerable (excluded children – sometimes now interpreted as unsophisticated people who often understand the truth), the needy (excluded from the rich man's view of faith), and newness (as the disciples too are thinking along the old lines of privilege through supposed close connection with the divine).

The final major section (11-15), a quarter of the gospel, is Jesus' last week, from the laying of palm branches in his honour to the utter contrast of degradation in his death. Again, alongside the dramatic story events there are *responses* to challenges and questions which come in two ways: concerned with his nature, person and authority from people who want him out of the way (often met with silence or counter-questions), and those concerned with his teaching – often from the same people but dealt with in a different way. The classic example is the question about the greatest Commandment; as before it is the Principle (loving God and neighbour) rather than the rules which is important; though Jesus is not silent about rules, as in the previous section where he condemns adultery, but with an added element of gender equality.

His other *responses* in the final chapters come together between 12:41 and 13:37. There are straightforward questions about future persecution and the destruction of the Temple, to which he adds the lesson of the fig tree and the coming of the Son of Man. But immediately preceding this is the story of the widow's mite (12:41-44). There is an obvious link to his own self-sacrifice, and the story is clearly designed and placed at this point to show the parallels for all people. In the twenty-first century it is still true that the poor give relatively more of their income to charity than the wealthy.

APPENDIX B

Additional notes for Chapter 10, Assisted Suicide

Church of England and Roman Catholic response to 2004 House of Lords bill.

1. The arguments presented in this submission grow out of our belief that God himself has given to humankind the gift of life. As such, it is to be revered and cherished.
2. Christian beliefs about the special nature and value of human life lie at the root of the Western Christian humanist tradition, which remains greatly influential in shaping the values held by many in our society. These beliefs are also shared in whole or in part by many people of all faiths and none.
3. All human beings are to be valued, irrespective of age, sex, race, religion, social status or their potential for achievement.
4. Those who become vulnerable through illness or disability deserve special care and protection. Adherence to this principle provides a fundamental test as to what constitutes a civilised society.
5. The whole of humankind is the recipient of God's gift of life. Life is to be received with gratitude and used

responsibly. Human beings each have their own distinct identities, but these are formed by and take their place within complex networks of relationships. All decisions about individual lives bear upon others with whom we live in community.

6. For this reason, the law relating to euthanasia is not simply concerned either with private morality or with utilitarian approaches. This is one of the issues – relatively few in number but fundamental in importance – on which justice calls for a limit to moral or ethical pluralism. A positive choice has to be made by society in favour of protecting the interests of its vulnerable members even if this means limiting the freedom of others to determine their end.

APPENDIX C

The Motor Neurone Disease (MND) Association funds and promotes research to bring about an end to MND. Until then, it does all that it can to enable everyone with MND to receive the best care, achieve the highest quality of life possible, and die with dignity. The MND Association will also do all that it can to support the families and carers of people with MND.

The MND Association has a support and information service, MND Connect, which provides equipment and financial grants and influences and educates health and social care professionals. If you would like further information please contact: 01604 250505, www.mndassociation.org